Praise for *How Fargo of You*:

"*How Fargo of You* **surprised and stretched me**, taking me to a place I've never been, giving me new lessons in what it means to be civilized. Marc de Celle has written a funny, profound book, showing how America can succeed in the 21st Century. An enlightening delight."

> — **Joel Barker,** *Paradigms: The Business of Discovering the Future, The Star Thrower Story, Future Edge,* others

"**A gifted writer reminds us of the remarkable people and stories that make America great.** With most of the emphasis on bad news these days, it is refreshing to read a book that spotlights the unique and wonderful things that happen around us every single day – moments the people of the Northern Prairie are truly gifted at making."

> — **Senator Byron Dorgan**

"**This is the perfect book to share with anyone who has ever asked you, 'Why do you live in Fargo?'**"

> — **Madalyn Pezella,** *Village Family Magazine*

"*How Fargo of You* **made me laugh out loud with tears in my eyes!** Marc de Celle gives the world an inside view of Northern Prairie Culture seldom seen by outsiders, while reminding those of us who call Fargo home why we're so lucky to live here."

> — **Kerstin Kealy, Anchor, WDAY TV, Fargo**

Close Encounters of the Fargo Kind
True Stories from a
Kind, Happy Little Planet
In America

www.fargokind.com

First Edition, First Printing
November 2013

ISBN 978-0-9830928-3-4

Close Encounters of the

Fargo Kind

To Charlene,
Anastasia and Austen.

In honor of all the contributors who gave their stories freely, one dollar of the proceeds from this book will be donated evenly amongst these ten charities in the Red River Valley:

- Ronald McDonald House of the Red River Valley
- CHARISM
- HERO
- Red River Zoo
- Jeremiah Program
- American Red Cross – Minn-Kota Region
- Fargo Moorhead Rotary Foundation
- Great Plains Food Bank
- Mayville State University Foundation
- Bras on Broadway

Thank you, storytellers.

Contents

INTRODUCTION

A Different Planet

This isn't the one I grew up on.

It was like landing on a different planet with a different species.

Fargo was only 1,800 miles from Phoenix, but it might as well have been 1,800 light years. When my family and I moved here in 2005, teenagers we'd never met helped us move in. Young children ran around freely, playing in their neighborhoods in complete safety. The local news was mostly **good.** We had to pump before we could pay! A carpenter I hired insisted the great job he did was *a housewarming gift.* When I made a mistake and had to cut someone off in traffic, instead of road rage, I got a friendly smile and a wave ahead (from a big guy in a large pickup wearing a cowboy hat, no less!) A couple we didn't know bought my son and I dinner, leaving the restaurant before we had any idea what they'd done or who they were...

That was just the beginning. The first important political debate I heard was so friendly and smart, I couldn't tell which candidate was the Republican and which was the Democrat. Then I watched 10,000 volunteers come out in force on less than a day's notice, making and placing more than a million sandbags in a week, saving the city from certain disaster. Weirdest of all, I discovered that local bankers had refused to profit from Wall Street's "creative mortgage products," so Fargo never had a "Mortgage Meltdown," and sidestepped the Great Recession. (Fargo's economic boom has almost nothing to do with the oil patch, 300 miles away, supplied and run mostly out of Texas and Oklahoma. But that's a story you'll read later.)

In short, Fargo was not the planet I'd spent my first fifty years on. It was an entirely different species of culture than I'd ever imagined possible. I had no idea human beings could behave this way, en masse, and I couldn't get over the fact that this place actually existed, that it was *real*. It seemed, much of the time, like I was living in a fairy tale, an *Opposite World* from the one I'd known before.

So I wrote a book about it. **How Fargo of You** was titled after an expression I'd come up with, because I was constantly finding myself tongue-tied and speechless. "Thank you" was regularly inadequate. "How nice of you" didn't cut it.

For instance, I accidentally knocked my coke over in a convenience store this last summer, making a big mess. Not only did the cashier immediately come to my aid, but a young lady who didn't work there pitched in, too. Then, before I knew what was going on, the young lady paid for my coke and the hot dog I'd been about to buy and left the store! When I found out from the cashier what she'd done, I ran out to the parking lot just in time to stop her as she was pulling out.

"That was so nice of you!" I said, a bit breathless, "But let me pay you back." I was pulling out my wallet.

"No!" she said emphatically, with a smile, shaking her head. "It's just something I like to do once in a while. Just pass it on, you know, pay it forward."

For a moment, I again found myself speechless. Then I said, "Well, how Fargo of you!"

"What?" she asked, with a puzzled look.

"How *Fargo* of you!" I repeated. "It's just an expression I use when someone around here does something outrageously generous and nice!"

She started laughing. "Don't worry about it! You looked like you could use a little pick-me-up."

"Yeah, like 'pick-me-up' my coke from all over the floor and then pay for it along with my hot dog without telling me!" I said.

She laughed again.

"What's your name?" I asked.

"Julia," she said, still smiling.

"Wait a minute; I have something I want to give you." I ran to my minivan and got a copy of *How Fargo of You* – I keep a stock with me at all times for just such emergencies – and wrote in it, "You helped clean up my mess – then bought me lunch! How Fargo of You!" then signed and gave it to her.

But writing *How Fargo of You* wasn't enough. It was just one family's story of moving here. People who don't already know Fargo might think my family was just ridiculously lucky, or that I was simply exaggerating. So I asked people who live around here to start sending me one or two of their Fargo stories – because everyone around here has more than a few.

Hundreds of people sent or told me a story or two. You're holding the result. By no means does this book contain all the stories I received or heard. But it's a good start.

At first, I thought I might rewrite these stories, putting them in third person and spiffing them up. That was a terrible idea. Choked the life out of the few I tried it on. So instead, I've done my best to edit them as they were written. You're hearing the voices of the people who told them.

I'm in these pages a bit, too. I introduce each new Book, of which there are four, and I've intermingled a few of my own stories throughout, some old and some new, when I thought they might help illuminate a certain aspect of this kind, happy planet my family now gratefully calls home.

I hope you enjoy these Close Encounters of the Fargo Kind.

Marc de Celle,
November 6, 2013

Warning: Don't Get All Excited and Move to Fargo

If you've never visited the Northern Prairie, you are about to enter a different world in these pages. You will probably react the way most of us do, on first contact: disbelief, then amazement, then wonder. Who knew human beings could behave like this?

But don't get all excited and just move to Fargo. Less than a year ago, a woman who runs a local charity for homeless children told me of a man living in the southern U.S. who'd heard about Fargo, left his job and moved his family here. They ended up in the homeless shelter this last Fargo winter.

This is not a good place to be homeless in the winter.

Like all alien cultures – which the Northern Prairie is, to the rest of the country, at this point – this one has many nuances that novices can trip over, falling flat on their faces.

First, read this entire book. You'll pick up a few good pointers here and there. Second, come for a visit and see for yourself if you like it here. Then last, and most important, if you decide you want to live *anywhere* in the Northern Prairie, unless you have a big pile of cash stashed away, get a good job offer *first, before you come.* We have quite a few jobs hanging around, but they aren't as pluckable as you might think, for reasons that will probably surprise you. They certainly surprised me.

Read on.

Book I

Anonymous Kindness

Life is full of surprises.
Create as many good ones as you can.

1.

Signature Acts

Written in invisible ink.

I've come to think of this as the secret, unseen trademark of this wonderfully strange world my family and I landed on eight years ago: Anonymous Kindness. An unknown stranger coming to the rescue, in circumstances ranging from dire to comical, no names exchanged, just help freely given. Often, the face of the unknown benefactor is never seen.

I had no idea how deep this went until the release of my first book, *How Fargo of You*, where I detailed some of the many acts of Anonymous Kindness my family and I had been at the receiving end of since we'd moved here. That book opened the floodgates – people started telling me their stories all the time. It soon became clear that Anonymous Kindness is a staple of life around here, but no one talks about it much, unless you write a book about it.

I remember an elderly couple at one of my first book signings, telling me a story. They'd been leaving a restaurant, and the woman had dropped her purse in the snowy parking lot, probably while getting into the car. But they had no idea her purse was even missing, until they got home and listened to the answering machine. The manager of the restaurant had called, telling them he had her purse. It had immediately been discovered by a patron arriving for dinner, who had taken it into the manager. The manager had then looked at the ID in the wallet and called. The husband drove back and retrieved it. Everything inside was untouched.

"Oh, what a great story!" I remember saying. "When did that happen?"

"Oh, that was just a couple of nights ago," the man said.

"Yes, that was Wednesday night," the lady added, nodding.

I remember being surprised. I expected to start hearing a few Fargo stories after the book came out, of course. But I didn't expect they'd so often be about something that had just happened.

But then, I did some simple math, and suddenly it all made sense. I knew I'd experienced between five and ten acts of

Anonymous Kindness every year since we'd moved to Fargo, from getting towed out of snow banks within seconds of becoming stuck to Julia, who I didn't know at the time, buying my hot dog and coke after I made a mess at the convenience store this last summer.

Well, if it's normal for a person to experience just five acts of Anonymous Kindness every year around here – and it is, I believe – and there are a little over 200,000 people living in the Fargo area, then something like a million acts of Anonymous Kindness must happen in the immediate vicinity every year! Here's the basic math:

5 Acts of Anonymous Kindness annually per person
x 210,000 people
1,050,000 acts of Anonymous Kindness every year
within about a ten-mile radius of downtown Fargo.

Divided by 365 days, that's close to three thousand acts of Anonymous Kindness every day!

Even if I'm off by 50%, that's outrageous. Definitely not the planet I grew up on.

No wonder the locals tend to usually remember only the most recent iteration of Fargo they've experienced, and those are the stories I most often hear.

There's undoubtedly one happening right now, as you read this. Probably two or three.

2.

First Night in Town

"I found myself surrounded by giant, bearded Norsemen."

This might be my favorite story of Fargoan Anonymous Kindness. I've told it before, and I'll tell it again. Right now.

"Hi, caller, what's your name?" I was sitting across from Dan Michaels, morning DJ for the *Eagle* radio station in Fargo. My book **How Fargo of You** had just been released, and Dan had asked his listeners to call in with their own Fargo stories. The switchboard instantly lit up like a Christmas tree, and Dan was taking the first call.

"My name's Lou, and I just got into town last week, and I had my first Fargo experience the first night I got into town."

"Well, what happened, Lou?" Dan asked.

"Well, I've never driven in snow before…"

"Oooooh," I cringed involuntarily, and all three of us started laughing. It was December, and Fargo's streets had been icy most of the month. I looked at Dan. "I gotta hear this."

"Yeah, well," Lou continued, still chuckling, "so as soon as I got into town I got stuck in a snow bank on Broadway…"

More laughter all around. By now, I could detect that Lou had some kind of southern accent.

"So then what happened, Lou?" Dan was still smiling.

"Well, it was about seven at night and it was already dark out, and I wasn't sure what to do. The nearest thing I saw open was a bar called the Bismarck…"

Dan and I erupted in laughter. Lou was chuckling, too. The Bismarck, at the north end of downtown Fargo, has a reputation for harboring what can best be described as 21st Century Viking types. But Lou, upon arriving, wouldn't have known that.

"So I went in," Lou continued, "and I gotta tell you, I'm a black guy from Louisiana, so I wasn't sure what to expect…"

Dan and I glanced at each other.

"…and I suddenly found myself surrounded by giant, bearded Norsemen…"

Dan and I lost it again.

"So what happened then?" Dan asked as soon as he was able to speak.

13

"Well, I kind of quietly walked up to the bar," Lou said, "and I asked the bartender if he had a phone I could use, and he said sure, and pointed to the end of the bar where there was a phone. But then one of the big guys at the bar asked why I needed a phone, so I told him what had happened, and while I was explaining he pulled out his car keys and handed them to me! And he said... he said, 'Well, you can use my truck to get it out, it's got a strap in the back. It's the big red one parked right out front.'"

"Whoa!" I let out. "Now *that's* a *How Fargo of You* story!"

"Yeah, where I come from people don't just hand their car keys to strangers!" Lou was kind of yelling now, still clearly amazed by his first encounter with Fargo. "But I had no idea what to do, I mean, I've seen a couple people get pulled out of the snow since I got here so now I know what a strap is, that people carry them around to rescue each other out of snow banks. But when he held out his truck keys, I didn't take 'em. I mean, I was kinda stunned."

"I know what you mean, Lou," I said, "A lot of people like you and I, people who didn't grow up around here, are sort of in a state of shock after our first Fargo, uh, our first few Fargo experiences."

"So then what happened, Lou?" Dan asked.

"Well, then, one of the other bearded giants elbowed the guy with the keys and said, 'Don't make him pull his own car out!' And all of a sudden there were three big guys walking out the door asking where my car was. And they didn't need a truck or a strap. They just pushed me out of the snow bank like it was nothing, you know, three muscled-up young Santas."

"Well, Lou," Dan said through the laughter, "Welcome to Fargo!"

Now let's let some other people tell their stories.

3.

A Fargo Magic Trick

See the gloves disappear, then reappear magically.

I met my husband right after he moved here from Chicago for a job. He points out many "How Fargo" moments we experience, which apparently I don't notice and take for granted, having grown up here! I was just reminded of a particularly mysterious instance when getting out our winter gear the other day.

A few winters ago, we had gone shopping at West Acres Mall in Fargo. When we got home, however, my husband realized he'd lost his very nice leather gloves I had just given him for Christmas. We were bummed, but didn't bother going back. We had been all over the mall, and figured someone just scored a nice new pair of gloves.

The next week, a large padded envelope (with no return address!) arrived in the mail. Hmmmm... A late Christmas gift from someone, we thought? We opened it to find my husband's leather gloves! The only thing we could figure out is that he left them at the checkout counter at one of the stores where we had purchased something with a store credit card account, and some kindly employee actually looked up our address and mailed them to us!

After getting over the shock that a complete stranger working retail during the busy holiday season actually took the time and effort to return the gloves, we had a good laugh and, as he often does, my husband exclaimed, "ONLY in Fargo!"

Tammy Enright, Fargo

4.

Many Happy Returns

These happen all the time around here.

I grew up on the central coast of California, living there for thirty years. But my father was born in Williston, North Dakota, and still has a lot of family members scattered throughout that part of the country. So occasionally we would visit the region for family reunions.

One year, there was going to be a family reunion near Detroit Lakes, Minnesota, about an hour east of Fargo, where much of my dad's family had spent time in their youth. I was taking some summer college classes and could only get away for a short while, but Detroit Lakes is beautiful in the summer, and these family reunions are a lot of fun, so I decided to go anyway.

The plane landed in the Twin Cities and we drove up to the Detroit Lakes area, arriving late in the evening. The family reunion was at a large resort, with lots of other people around as well as our family. Soon, everyone was drinking beer and playing volleyball, and the fun lasted into the wee hours of the morning; then everyone crashed.

I woke up about 9 a.m., and quickly realized I didn't have my man purse! It contained everything I owned: $300 cash, plane tickets home, driver's license, checkbooks, camera and more! You get the picture. I grew up in Salinas, California, where you couldn't leave your car unlocked, and even if you did, it could still get broken into; I'd had my car broken into twice in my life up to that date. So I was immediately expecting that I was probably going to have to hitch-hike my way back to California, miss my midterm, fail my class and lick my wounds... but on the off chance, I decided to go to the front desk of the resort where we were staying. I walked in and asked if they had heard of a bag that I had "lost" the night before. The nice girl at the counter asked if I was Brian and knew exactly what bag I was talking about! She then handed it to me! I figured there was no way everything was still in there, but I was hoping for at least an ID and some plane tickets

I opened it, checked around, and couldn't believe it. *Everything* was just as I had left it!

I was beyond words, but the response from the girl behind the counter was what drove me beyond comprehension: "Why wouldn't it be as you left it?"

About twenty minutes later, after the shock wore off, I decided I needed to move. I've been living in the Northern Midwest ever since, and never plan on going back to California.

To this day I can't hardly recount that story without getting teary eyed. God bless the people out here, they are truly amazing.

Brian McLaughlin, Edina, Minnesota

Editor's Note: On December 4, 2012, Valley News Live (a local television news team) ran a story about Jacob Boucher of Fargo, who accidentally dropped his wallet on the sidewalk in downtown Fargo. It had his girlfriend's half of the rent money in it, credit cards and ID.

But he didn't realize it was missing. Until his cell phone rang. It was the Fargo Police Department, telling him to come pick it up. Everything was there.

What's great about this story – which has no byline – is that Valley News Live then did a brief interview with Deputy Chief Todd of the Fargo Police Department, who talked about how this happens all the time here, and the people bringing in the lost wallet or purse or whatever "are giving it to us so that we can give it to the person and restore their life, in effect."

He then added that these submissions to the Police Department are almost always made anonymously.

The story ended with this note: *Recently, someone turned in a very expensive necklace that was found at West Acres Mall, and police are hoping to get it back to its rightful owner. If it's yours, they say to give them a call and tell them the approximate time and date it was lost.*

5.

Turning Disaster into Wonder

Another mysterious Fargo trick.

My family and I were deeply affected by the Grand Forks flood of 1997, which wiped out tens of thousands of homes. When it came time for the evacuation, our family had to leave and live in our camper at the air base for a week. When my parents, with three children, ages 6, 14 and 16, were finally able to return and see how much water damage we had (the whole basement was filled with water) they decided to move our family to Fargo for a month. We stayed at the Ramada Inn.

When things were finally fixed up enough for us to move back to Grand Forks, we packed up and my parents went to pay the bill. They knew it would be in the thousands.

But instead, they were told it had been taken care of. All they were able to find out was that a lady doctor – who to this day my parents do not know the name of or what she looks like – had offered to help a family who was affected by the flood and paid our full hotel bill for us.

I am stationed in Hawaii, and even though it is sunny here almost every day, it never compares to the sense of community we have back home. Your stories always brighten my day!

ITSN Alexander, Miranda L.
COMPACFLT
N310 Fleet Command Center

6.

Warmth of the Fargo Kind

Moving from Key West, Florida, to warm up.

We just moved back to this area a few weeks ago, in the middle of winter! We're just sixty miles east of Fargo, in Detroit Lakes, Minnesota. The Lakes country! But right now, they're mostly hard and white!

Can you imagine what our Key West friends were saying, seeing us move from there to here at this time of year?

"Why now? Why not wait until spring, at least?"

I actually began to wonder if we were making the right decision. We'd already raised our kids in Fargo and moved eleven years ago to 'warmth' – but we'd always come back in the summers, sometimes just for a few weeks, others the whole summer. I was really wondering, but as soon as we arrived a few weeks ago, I immediately felt 'at home' and happy. You can't find a better place to be happy! I keep commenting on facebook (for my Key West friends) how wonderful it is here. The cold can be dealt with - it's the PEOPLE that make this place fantastic.

Here's a recent example. It's a facebook post I saw about a week ago, from Norby's Department Store in Detroit Lakes. After reading your book, *How Fargo of You*, I went back to facebook and copied this so I could pass it on:

<u>Norby's Department Store</u>: Karen in our kids' dept just shared the sweetest story. A woman and her daughter were buying a Christmas dress...and when it came to the sparkly tights that matched it perfectly, the mother wasn't too sure about the expense and decided not to get them. Well, the lady behind her at the register decided that little girl needed to complete the outfit & bought them for her! A little bit of Christmas spirit shared... pass it on!

Doesn't get much warmer than that, anywhere on earth!

Barb Herzog, Detroit Lakes, Minnesota

7.

A Good Man

*A single act of kindness can have an influence for life,
and other lives beyond.*

I want to tell you of a good man and the influence he had on me. I have lived in North Dakota all my life and am now 61 years old. I first met Martin Seifert when my brother Mike dated his niece, before they got married.

I was deer hunting with a cousin and a friend near his farm at Hettinger, North Dakota when we ran into a ditch during a sleet storm. I knew where Martin's farm was, and we were able to walk there through the storm. Martin and his wife made their home available to us for the night, provided dinner for us that evening and put us up . The next morning, we all received a hearty breakfast before leaving to retrieve my car.

Martin then drove one of his tractors over and pulled us out. When I tried to pay him, he refused. He told me that to repay him, I would have to help someone else, and that would be his pay – and that only I would know if I had made the payment.

I have always remembered what he said and have tried to do exactly as he told me. I have taught my daughter and son the same thing and they are willing to help people and to not take any payment and to tell people to help someone else and that is the pay. Martin's tale to me took place 40 years ago long before Pay it Forward came about and I like to think this my way of giving him credit for being able to realize that what he inspired was my *How Fargo of You* incident and I did not have a name for it, but I do now.

Alex Neigum, Mandan, ND

8.

He Looked at Me Like I Was from Mars

Asking what I owed him was not the thing to say.

I moved here in June of 1974 from Ohio. We moved in a 20 foot cab-over truck.. I had never driven anything like that out on the road. It was an experience.

After unloading the truck at the farm we were moving into, I headed into town. Suddenly, I hit a frost boil in the road. I tried to move over toward the edge of the road to gain traction, but instead, slipped into the ditch and got stuck. I only knew our closest neighbor, so I started to walk back toward his house, when along came a pickup with that very neighbor in it! (I almost wonder if he'd been following me at a safe distance "just in case...")

He stopped and looked at the truck, and as we were discussing how to get it out, another pickup stopped. Then another. Soon there was a gathering of neighbors! Doesn't take long to meet all your neighbors around here, even though they might live miles away!

One guy backed his truck up to mine and pulled out a chain that had been repaired a few times, with bolts and nuts holding it together, and hooked it up to my truck. I was a little leery of the setup, but being an "outsider," I didn't say anything, just got in my truck. He pulled me out without a problem.

I got out and thanked him, then asked what I owed him. He looked at me like I was from Mars. I don't remember exactly what he said, but it was clear that asking what I owed him was not the thing to say.

Where I'd come from, if you could get someone to pull you out – a big "if" – he probably would have said, "Maybe twenty bucks."

That was my first "How Fargo of you" experience, but certainly not the last. As you know, they happen all the time around here!

I could probably write a book about all our experiences. But I'll let you do that!

Terry Mickunas, Sebeka, Minnesota

9.

Give that Family a Pass

Passing on the passing on.

Just prior to Christmas, my wife and I stopped out at the Red River Zoo. We were there to purchase a family pass for her brother's family for the coming year. While I poked around the lobby, my wife handled the transaction. After what seemed an inordinate amount of time, she approached me and said, "Someone ahead of us paid for the next person's family pass."

I asked, "What did you do?"

She said, "I just paid for ours and let the freebie go to the next person."

Here's a case where kindness was met with humility, and illustrates the synergistic nature of selfless acts. It could have ended at the one purchase.

But my wife, in her 'we-really-aren't-that-needy' way, passed along the grace of an anonymous donor to yet another anonymous recipient, thereby relaying benevolence beyond even the original person's intent.

Keith Corliss, West Fargo

10.

Two More Happy Returns

I'm tellin' ya. This happens a lot.

I've had two instances where I've lost something in Fargo and had it returned.

The first was three years ago. I was in a shopping center parking lot, getting my kids buckled into their car seats. I had set my purse on the roof of my car, but in the hustle and bustle of kids and groceries, I then forgot it was there. It was only after returning home I realized it was missing and what I had done.

I drove back to the store where we'd been shopping. First I searched the parking lot, with no luck. Then I took the same route home, looking alongside the streets. Still no luck. Arrrrw.

Then, about a week later, I received a package in the mail. Someone had found my purse and mailed it back to me! Everything was perfectly intact, of course!

Then last fall, I lost my phone at the Hub, a local concert club. Over the next couple of days, I called them several times to see if it had been turned in, with no luck.

But three days after losing it, I came home from work to find my phone on the front porch, with a note saying "Found your phone, I hope you enjoyed the concert despite losing it!"

I was never able to thank the people who helped me. Both returns were completely anonymous. But both times I thought, "Wow! There are sure are good people around here!"

Sholauna Stautz, Fargo

11.

Lookin' Out for the Old Guy

Very basic. But very important.

My husband suffers from Parkinson's and dementia, and we constantly experience people going out of their way to give our lives an added glow.

When we attend sporting events our granddaughter is in, for instance, young people will dash to open the door and help Tom up into the bleachers. People who have arrived at the game early, to get that special place to sit, almost always offer up their seats as soon as they see Tom come into the gym, with his shuffling gate. At one high school event, out of town, but in the area, Tom reached the door and was holding it open. Usually when this happens, people take the door from him and say, "You go ahead". But this particular game, a 40-something gentleman said, "Well, thank you" and entered. My eyes filled with tears when, with pride, Tom said, "You're welcome, glad I could help."

I caught up with the gentleman and said "Thank you, that was so kind of you to let him hold the door for you."

He simply said, with a kindly smile, "My Dad had Parkinson's."

Margaret Ann Thompson, Barnesville, Minnesota

12.

Another Happy Return

By the time you know it's lost, it isn't.

In September of 2011, I was traveling from my home in Belle Fourche, South Dakota to spend a week with my two sisters in Fargo and Wyndmere, North Dakota. I was taking my usual route for this trip, what I refer to as the road of the Five "B"s; Belle Fourche, Buffalo, Bowman, Belfield and Bismarck, then on to Fargo. I usually stop at each of these places to get gas, buy a snack or just get out of the car. When I got to Bowman, North Dakota, I did stop to get a snack, and discovered that my Pioneer Bank debit card was missing.

I pride myself in being a very calm person in the face of urgency. Of course, that does not make it true. I instantly went into panic mode. Where is it?? I dumped out my purse, not once, not twice, but three times, searching every pocket and crevice. Not there. I looked under and between the seats, front and back. Not there. I combed the glove compartments and visors. Not there. I lifted the hatch and went through my entire luggage, just to make sure I did not slip it into my overnight bag. Not there. Every pocket of my jeans and jacket was thoroughly and repeatedly searched. Not there! Horrific scenarios were wreaking havoc in my mind; identity theft, purchases made that would not require the PIN, and worst of all, my husband being able to say, "So you think you are responsible, do you remember the debit card incident of September, 2011?"

Meanwhile, kindhearted (and probably curious) folks are approaching me and asking if something is wrong, and asking if they can help me. Here is where the fake calmness kicks in, "No, thank you, I am just fine," I would reply.

I finally faced reality; I must have left it at my last stop, the previous "B", Henderson Oil and Convenience Store in Buffalo, South Dakota. Finding the phone number on the receipt from Henderson Oil Co. (sure, I could find that!), I called my husband, Doug, in Belle Fourche to ask him to call Henderson Oil and see if anyone had turned in my card. I knew it was a long shot. I would more than likely have to report it stolen, and wait for a new card. Like so many of us, I have really come to depend on the convenience of my debit card.

I have to admit, I was not looking forward to my husband hinting at my carelessness with something so valuable. I took a deep breath when dialing him.

Much to my surprise, he answered the phone, "Hi, JoAnn, looking for your debit card?"

The story he then proceeded to tell me relays the honesty and integrity of the people involved. First, the card dropped to the ground when I was getting into my car and was found by a perfect stranger, who picked it up and brought it into the convenience store attendant on duty. Next, that Henderson Oil Co. employee took the initiative to call the local Buffalo branch of Pioneer Bank, speaking to Vicky, the branch manager. God bless her, she left the bank and drove out to Henderson's, got the card and returned to the bank with it. She then looked up our information, found our number and called my husband to let him know my card had been found and would be coming to our branch, the Belle Fourche branch, the next day, via carrier, at no charge. All this had happened before I'd even realized my card was gone! She just needed to know who we wished to receive it at the Belle Fourche branch. A neighbor and friend, Lee Voyles was elected, who in turn, hand delivered it to Doug. The card was back home in less than 24 hours after it was lost.

All *is* well that ends well. There was no need for cancellation. No paperwork was necessary. No scolding from my husband came my way. Total cost to me; a near mini-stroke and some good natured teasing. Thanks to the kindness and trustworthiness of four people, three of whom I have never met,

I was able to travel on to Fargo and enjoy my week's stay with my sisters, knowing all is well in the Lange household in Belle Fourche, South Dakota.

JoAnn Lange, Belle Fourche, South Dakota

13.

It Could Have Been the Worst Day

But was turned into the best, anonymously, face to face.

Like everyone around here, I have a number of Fargo stories, but there is one that surpasses all the others. Here it is.

It was graduation day at Moorhead State University, just across the river from Fargo, in May of 1993. My husband was graduating in the afternoon. We were also planning a move sixty miles north to Grand Forks, and I had a job interview and an appointment for an apartment rental there in the morning. It was going to be a busy day for me, driving up to Grand Forks, making my two appointments, then driving back down in time to attend my husband's graduation.

It was a fine sunny day, perfect for a drive. I got up early, dressed in a nice white dress, got in my car and drove away on I-29 North. I was excited and nervous but optimistic – until I got to Cass County Road 20, just north of Fargo, and my car died. It just stopped accelerating!

I had no idea what to do. I pulled over onto the shoulder and sat there a minute. Then I got out and put the hood up, not having a clue what to look for. And what would I do if I did? I mean, me in a white dress. Well, as I'm getting ready to walk to the nearest whatevericanfind, an older gentleman rolls up in a big RV. He pulls up in front of me and gets out of his vehicle.

What's wrong?" he asked.

"I have no clue, it just won't accelerate."

"Where were you going?"

I started telling him about my appointments in Grand Forks.

. "Hop in, I'll take you."

I was flabbergasted. "That's not necessary," I said. "I just need to get to a phone."

"I was headed to Page to see my brother, but now, given the choice, I think I'd rather spend the day with a pretty girl."

He was so genial it never crossed my mind that taking a ride from a stranger wasn't a good idea, and I got in. We chatted happily all the way to Grand Forks, although he never told me his name. He took me to my interview and waited for me in a coffee shop. When I was finished, he bought me breakfast and asked how it went.

Walking out of the coffee shop, we saw the RV had a flat tire. He quickly changed the tire, putting on a spare, then we went to a service station to get the other fixed. The whole time, we were smiling and chatting away, as if this happened all the time! I offered to pay for getting his tire fixed – it wouldn't have happened if he hadn't been acting as my personal chauffeur – but he refused.

After the tire was fixed, he took me to my apartment rental appointment and waited for me. I finished that appointment at about 1:30 in the afternoon. My husband's graduation ceremony sixty miles south in Moorhead was scheduled to start at 3:00.

We stopped to gas up, and while he was at the pump I went into the station and paid for the gas. When he later went in to pay and found out I had beat him to it, he came out and insisted on paying me the money back! I told him it was the least I could do for his incredible kindness, but he refused to hear it, saying it was totally unnecessary.

Driving back to Fargo, we continued chatting and enjoying the ride. Not far out of Fargo he asked where the graduation ceremony was taking place, and he drove me right to the front door of the Nemzek Fieldhouse on the MSU campus.

I asked him his name one last time so that I could thank him properly, and he said "It doesn't matter, just pay it forward." That was years before the movie!

I try to do just that whenever I am able.

I made it inside to watch the ceremony, just in time to see my husband receive his diploma.

It's the most fantastic story I've ever been able to tell. If this amazingly good Samaritan ever happens to read this, I just want to say to him, "How Fargo of you!"

Ardith DuBord, Fargo

14.

Mayville

Getting to the heart of the matter.

I was just finishing up a two-hour book signing event in downtown Fargo. It was November of 2011, and the Third Edition of **How Fargo of You** had just been released.

And, as so often happens around here, my life was about to change.

A tall, pleasant-looking fiftysomething woman approached me. "Hello," the woman said, with an exceedingly gracious manner and tone, "my name is Professor Carolyn Baker." She placed three books on the table for me to sign, then we shook hands. "I'm hoping to talk with you about the possibility of working with some of my students at Mayville State University."

"That sounds interesting," I said, hesitating before signing her books. "Where is Mayville State?" I didn't want to commit to a lot of five-hour drives, which is easy to do in North Dakota.

"It's in Mayville, about sixty miles north-northwest of Fargo. It's just about thirty miles from Grand Forks, ten miles west of the Interstate."

That sounded doable. I often go to Grand Forks for book events, anyway. I noticed there was no one in line behind her – she'd obviously waited to approach.

"Why don't you have a seat?" I asked, motioning to the chair off to the side of the signing table.

"Oh, well, thank you," she said, and sat down.

"First, would you like these books signed to anyone in particular?"

We talked about who she would be giving the books to for Christmas, and I personalized them for her.

It was then that a great, unforeseen experiment began.

"I have an Intercultural Studies class made up of kids from around the country, and around the world," Dr. Baker explained, "and most of them have just arrived in our region. I was thinking it might be interesting to have each of them write their own Fargo-type stories, for possible inclusion in your next book."

"That sounds interesting," I said. "What would you like me to do?"

"Well, I'll have them all read your book, and then, if you would come up to the University at the beginning of the semester in January and talk with them about what you're looking for, that would be great. Then, at the end of the semester in May, you'd come back up again and I'll have them all present their stories to you."

And that's exactly what we did. Except for a hitch, which I created.

You see, I still didn't really get it. I still couldn't fully accept that this place was, for all practical purposes, like living on a different planet from the one I grew up on. I'd lived here six years, written a book about my first five, then marveled at all the stories I kept hearing from others during the year after the book was released.

But I still didn't get it. Not really. But Dr. Baker, her students and the town of Mayville were about to change that.

I suggested her students might want to help me polish some of the stories I'd already received from others. We agreed that if the students didn't have a personal experience they wanted to write about, I would arrange for them to help me turn some of the very rough stories I'd received into something more polished.

After all, these kids were brand new to the area. They were kids in a small town – Mayville has a population of less than two-thousand – all centered around a small university. They were probably living in dorms and intermingling with other students from other places, like themselves, for the most part. They certainly wouldn't all being experiencing something remarkable, a true "Fargo" story, something really worth writing about, in the few months between now and May.

So in early January of 2012, I rolled up to Mayville and met the small class of about a dozen kids. I told them the story of moving to Fargo and how I'd come to write the book, and answered questions about everything from writing techniques to the kind of research I might like them to do on some of the stories I'd already received. It was short, sweet and simple – except for the gracious hospitality I received from Dr. Baker and everyone else on campus, which was overflowing.

Over the next few weeks, there were some emails back-and-forth concerning some stories I might like some of the students to work on. But soon, that correspondence trickled off. *Oh, well. It will be interesting to hear the stories in May,* I thought to myself.

Little did I know.

On May first, 2012, Dr. Baker led me into the Luckasen Room on the campus of Mayville State University. In the middle of the room, seated in a semicircle, were her students, whose faces I recognized from January.

Dr. Baker had me sit down in front of them. She sat to my left. Then she turned to the large, young, African American student on the left end of the semicircle. "Trevin, why don't you start with your story, and we'll just go around the circle."

Trevin Tate is about six-foot-six, I'd guess, weighing in at something approaching three hundred pounds. I later learned he was attending Mayville on a football scholarship. Trevin proceeded to tell the story of Ardith DuBord's wonderful excursion up to Grand Forks in an RV with an unknown chauffeur, on her husband's graduation day in 1993, which you just read in the last chapter. Now by tell, I mean tell. This wasn't a formal reading. Trevin had his paper to hand, but he was simply recounting to me what he'd learned about Ardith's journey. (I had helped Trevin and Ardith connect at the beginning of the semester, asking Trevin to learn as many details about Ardith's voyage as he could.)

But, it was after Trevin finished that my amazement truly began. For all the students that followed Trevin had a remarkable story to tell that had happened to them, or friends of theirs, in just the last few months! (And I learned from Trevin later he also had such a story to tell, but when it happened, he had already committed to telling Ardith's story.)

Sit in with me now, as we go around the semicircle, and listen to each of these students describe their own stories of Anonymous Kindness.

15.

Rachel's Story

Getting accustomed to a different cultural climate.

"Okay, Rachel," Dr. Baker said, looking at an attractive blonde lady in her late twenties sitting just to Trevin's left – she was the second person in on the Intercultural Studies semicircle – "Why don't you share your story with Marc?"

"Hi, I'm Rachel Knoedler," the blonde lady said with a smile, "and my husband, Paul, is in the Air Force, and he was transferred to the Grand Forks Air Force Base from Okinawa about six months ago, so that's when we came to North Dakota.

And almost as soon as we got here, we bought a home, our first home, in downtown Grand Forks.

When we were moving in, the neighbors introduced themselves right away and were very friendly. We've moved a lot in the military, and even on military installations, we've rarely had neighbors come over so quickly and be so helpful and friendly, and we noticed that right away.

"Anyway, one morning after our first heavy snowfall, Paul noticed he would have to shovel the walkway when he got home from work. But when he got home, the snow from the walkway had already been removed. So, being first-time homeowners, we just guessed that the city must be doing the snow removal for homeowners, as part of our property taxes or something.

"Anyway, about a week later, the same thing happened again. Another heavy snow fell again and, sure enough, after work, the snow was gone! We thought it was a pretty nice perk to home ownership here! We never gave it a second thought.

"Anyway, about a week after that, Paul was taking our dogs on their nightly neighborhood walk. The weather was in the upper twenties and snowflakes were falling, and near the end of his walk, he noticed one of our neighbors out riding his snowplow, clearing the sidewalk around his house.

"As Paul passed by, the neighbor asked if he wanted him to plow Paul's sidewalks and walkways. Paul said he appreciated the offer, but he was content just waiting for the city to get to it.

"The neighbor looked a little confused and told my husband that the city only does it if you don't take care of it yourself, and for a corner lot, which is what we have, they would charge about a hundred and fifty dollars and just tack it on to our property taxes at the end of the year! My husband was shocked! He told me he also felt pretty embarrassed to have been so naïve.

"So he told the neighbor he'd had no idea that the city was charging him anything and had just assumed that the city was including the removal in what he already paid for property taxes.

"The neighbor thought that was pretty funny and laughed, and just said 'nope.'

"So my husband then told the neighbor he'd be grateful if he could remove the snow just this one time, so he didn't get charged another hundred and fifty dollars, as it had already been removed twice, costing him three hundred dollars!

"Then the neighbor said, 'Oh, no, I did that. Since you just moved to North Dakota, I figured you didn't know you had to remove it. '"

"Paul was shocked again! The neighbor had never said anything about it. Paul had never seen this kind of behavior in all his Air Force travels. He offered to pay the neighbor, but the man refused, saying he'd done it just to help out, not to make money or anything like that.

"We've lived in seven different states due to Paul's job in the Air Force, and outside the country, too, but we had never experienced that kind of altruistic helping before we moved to Grand Forks. We'd heard, when we were moving to North Dakota, that it was a tight-knit community that really pulled together and helped each other. But then we got to experience it right away, in just our first month here!"

16.

North Dakota Vendettas

They're hard to avoid.

Once Rachel finished her story, we chatted for a minute about how different North Dakota was from all the places she and her husband had lived before. Then I remembered a story.

"Oh, I have to tell you my favorite snowblowing story," I said. "I heard this from Brian Johnson of Arthur, just about thirty miles south of here. [1]

---

[1] You can read a story about Brian, *Quit Fargoing Me Up!* In Book I, *The Fargo Way.*

"Brian had known a lady who'd grown up in the area, he'd told me, but who'd moved away after graduating, pursuing a career somewhere far from North Dakota. But then, many years later when she retired, she moved back. People from North Dakota often move back to the cold to retire."

"Yeah, to warm up!" one of the kids said, and everyone laughed.

"Yeah," I nodded, chuckling. "Anyway, during the years she'd been away, this lady had apparently grown accustomed to sleeping in, which, by Dakota standards, meant she normally got up about seven or eight in the morning.

"After she moved in, the first time it snowed overnight, her driveway was cleared when she woke up. She asked around, but couldn't find out who had done it.

"When it snowed again, it happened again. And again, she couldn't find out who had done it.

"And it kept happening over and over again. For two years! Finally, one night when she knew it was going to snow, she set her alarm for four in the morning or something like that, and she finally caught the culprit, one of her neighbors, quietly shoveling her driveway at five in the morning!

"It took two years to catch him! Then she had to bake him cookies for a couple of years to catch up.

Dr. Baker's class got a good laugh out of that story, encouraging me immensely. They were supposed to be telling me their stories, but I couldn't help myself.

"Over the last couple of years, I've heard aabout a dozen snowblowing stories. One guy told me of an odd 'snow-blowing triangle' on his block, where he was snowblowing someone else's driveway in secret, but that person became convinced it was someone else on the block doing it, so he started surreptitiously snowblowing that person's driveway, and then that third person thought it was the first person – the fellow who was telling me the story – who was doing those good deeds, so started snowblowing his driveway, and the guy who was telling me the story was pretty sure he'd figured it out, but he was pretty sure the other two still hadn't.

"I call this a 'North Dakota Vendetta.'" The group cracked up. "That's when someone else has done something extra nice for you, and now you've got to get busy and figure out a way to get back at them. Everybody has them around here. Usually a lot of them. They're hard to avoid."

17.

David's Story

"Things like this don't happen in San Diego."

After Rachel's story, Dr. Baker continued around the semicircle of her students, left to right, having each one in turn tell me his or her story.

There was David Fuerte, a young Hispanic man from San Diego, who told the story of how he and three of his friends, who all drove up together from San Diego, lost their "wheels" shortly after arriving in Mayville.

"So the five of us came up from San Diego," David explained, "But then our friend Manny, who had the car we drove up in, started thinking Mayville wasn't for him. He was very popular back in the 'hood, you know, and his mind was made up, he was going back. With him leaving so randomly, the four of us who stayed were stuck with nowhere to go, and no one to take us anywhere.

"We were miserable and in need of things from Grand Forks or Fargo, but we had no other choice but to stick it out, and do what we could do with what we had. I had always heard of college students experiencing these kinds of difficulties, but I never thought it would happen to me.

"But then, one day at dinner, a dorm mate from down the hall, who I later found out was named Dan Moore, overheard us talking with a few guys from the football team. He heard how we really needed stuff and had no car, and how we were struggling through our days. Surprisingly, without anyone saying anything to him, he offered to take us to Grand Forks if we wanted to go. I was dumbfounded to hear him ask such question, knowing that Grand Forks wasn't just down the street. It was a good drive to get there, about forty-five minutes or so.

"Taking him up on his offer gave us a chance to get to know this guy. We had never talked to Dan before, and yet he did such a nice thing for us, even though we were complete strangers! That had never happened to me in San Diego.

"Dan took all four of us to Grand Forks. We spent about two hours or so shopping at Walmart, buying everything that we needed, before heading back to Mayville. Dan was so patient! His attitude was extremely different than what I was accustomed to back home. In San Diego, most people wouldn't go out of their way to drive strangers around, then wait for them while they shopped!

"Surprising us even more, we found out that Dan was actually from Mayville. He had a dorm room he shared, but his family lived right down the street from the University. On the drive back, when we got into Mayville, he showed us where he and his family lived, and told us we were always welcome at his house!

"I had never seen anything like this before, you know, Dan didn't even really know us. Back at the dorms, we thanked him very much, and offered him money several times, but he refused to accept it and told us to save our money for another time we needed something from the store. Dan amazed me again, because back home, the majority of the people that I know would have at least asked for gas money or a favor in return.

"In San Diego, if you don't have a car, either you find a ride and give that person gas money, or you return the favor by doing something else.

"Dan didn't ask for either of these things from us. He was just a North Dakotan with such a warm heart for complete strangers, and he never expected anything back."

In the brief chat that followed David's story, I learned that David and his friends had subsequently had dinner with Dan and his parents at their house, and had a great time. "I didn't say anything about it because I'd already turned my story in when it happened."

18.

Justin's Story

"The nicest people I have ever met."

To David's left was a stocky, brown-haired kid. Dr. Baker just nodded toward him and he started in: "Hi, my name's Justin Dziedzic, and I'm from Brainerd, Minnesota," he said, in the fairly steady, even-toned way of speaking typical of most people who've grown up in central Minnesota (contrary to what the Cohen brothers would have you believe).

"I was walking outside on a really cold day last winter when my friend Seth came up and asked me if I wanted to come to his house for the weekend. It was a Friday, so I had been planning on relaxing in my dorm room, but Seth is a good friend, and he'd told me about his hometown, which was Forman, North Dakota, so I said I would. We both went to our dorms and packed stuff up, and pretty soon we were on the road.

"It was about a three hour drive. I was very tired and fell asleep. When I woke up, Seth said we were about an hour away. It felt like we were in the middle of nowhere. There were farms and flat lands everywhere.

"We then pulled up to a rusty old sign that read 'Forman, population 567.' An old run-down gas station was right next to the sign. I was beginning to get a little nervous about meeting his family, and living in their house for a couple days. As we pulled up to his two-storied beige colored house, he said "Make sure to take off your shoes once you get into the house!"

"I got out of the car and grabbed my bags.

"We walked up the steps to the front door and walked in his house. To my surprise, his entire family was waiting for us in the living room. I almost forgot to take off my shoes! His mom and dad, two younger brothers, and younger sister were there. They instantly took my bags, and welcomed me into their home. His grandma and grandpa were even there! Everyone was very, very nice.

"I had never been treated like this before as a guest. It was like I was a celebrity walking down a red carpet. They even had dinner waiting for us on the kitchen table!

"We sat down, and they told me to serve myself first. I dished myself up a plate, everyone else followed, and we talked a lot during dinner. They asked me a lot of questions about my life while we were eating. It was fun talking to them. They were the type of people that were really fun to talk to and get to know.

"When we were done eating, they took my plates to the sink for me. We then went downstairs. They had made a bed for me. They told me to help myself to the fridge downstairs. Seth and I then played some video games before he headed off to bed and I laid down and tried to go to sleep.

"But while I was laying there, trying to go to sleep, I thought to myself, 'These are the nicest people I have ever met!'"

19.

Friday the 13th

When bad luck turns to good.

"Alright Rahni," Dr. Baker intoned, looking at the young lady who was next in the semicircle.

"Well, the coldest winter day this year happened to be on January 13, 2012, which was a Friday the 13th." Unlike Rachel, David and Justin, this student was was looking at her notes, and reading from her article, which appeared to be several pages long. "Raven Smith and Jason Nozal, two Mayville students, decided that would be a good day to go get some winter apparel. They needed basic stuff like jackets and scarves."

"Excuse me, was it, uhh, Rahni?" I interrupted.

"Yeah?"

"What was the date?" I asked.

"January thirteenth," Rahni said.

"Of this year?"

"Yeah."

"And they didn't have jackets yet?"

"Well, Raven's from California."

The place erupted.

After I finished laughing, I said to the whole group, "Hey, I'm from California, too. It takes us a while to get North Dakota."

More laughter.

"Alright, Rahni. Sorry I interrupted. Go on."

Rahni went back to reading from her story:

"Well, for the trip to get winter clothes, Raven only wore a grey T-shirt and jean shorts and a pair of white tennis shoes. He was sure he could handle the weather, and he was doing pretty well. His friend Jason was from Minnesota, and wore a black long sleeve shirt and a pair of jean shorts as well – "

"Excuse me, Rahni?" Dr. Baker interrupted.

"Yeah?" she looked up at her professor, slightly worried.

"Why don't you just tell Mr. de Celle the story from what you learned. And this applies to everyone –" Dr. Baker was looking around the semicircle – "Mr. de Celle will get a copy of all your papers to take with him. For now, feel free to tell him your story in your own words, okay?"

Rahni shifted her gaze from the professor to me. "Well, these two guys, Raven and Jason, picked the coldest day of the year, and it was a Friday the thirteenth in January, to drive to Fargo to get winter clothes. And it was seventeen degrees below zero. And they were wearing shorts..."

More laughter from the group.

"...And after they left Mayville, Jason realized his gas light was on and he should have stopped for gas earlier..."

"Oh man," one of the kids in the semicircle said. Another spattering of laughter went around the semicircle of students.

"Anyway," Rahni continued, "even with the heater on they were cold, and then they ran out of gas about fifteen miles out of town, out in the middle of nowhere. And they were afraid they were going to freeze to death. But they had cell phones. So they had to decide who to call."

"Finally, Raven had an idea –"

"Uh-oh," I interrupted, loudly. The class cracked up again.

"No, this time it was a good idea," Rahni said. "He decided to call his friend Chaz, who lived in Fargo but was in Mayville that day, visiting his grandmother. As soon as Raven called Chaz, Chaz said he'd bring gas to them. Raven and Jason were very grateful, and told Chaz they'd give him thirty dollars, ten to pay for the gas he had offered to bring, and twenty to put gas in his own car.

"After about 20 minutes, Chaz pulled up behind Raven and Jason. By this time, Jason and Raven and Jason were really, really cold. People can freeze to death in cars when it's that cold. Anyway, they all got back to the gas station in Mayville, where Raven and Jason filled up and decided to try to still get to Fargo to buy winter clothes.

"Chaz made some joke to Raven about a 'North Dakotan' helping out the 'Cali' boy. They all had a good laugh, and Raven thanked Chaz and tried to pay him, but Chaz wouldn't accept the money.

"Chaz said 'I did it as a friend, not for a prize.'

"Raven tried very hard to get Chaz to take the money. Raven told him, 'It's the least I can do for saving our lives and taking away time you could've spent with your grandma.'

"He still declined the offer. Raven finally gave up. Raven and Jason set on their way. They set out to go get what they needed. Raven was now definitely persuaded he needed warmer clothes like Jackets, pants, and long-sleeved shirts.

"Raven was still a little confused, though. Even when he told me the story later, he still couldn't understand why Chaz wouldn't take the money. It occurred to him that he had some adjusting to do in North Dakota, and not just in his wardrobe!"

There was more laugher and commentary around the semicircle, which I won't repeat here.

It just wouldn't be very Fargo of me.

20.

Another Rescue

Happens a lot around here. People get accustomed to it,
to not being in charge of nature and helping each other deal.
Might be the most important thing.

"Hi, my name's Leah Greenlaw," started the next student in the semicircle, a very pretty brunette with a milky complexion.

"My story is from when I was a senior at Minot High School in North Dakota, and I went to pick up my friend Taylor on my way to school. That day was the last day I would be giving her a ride, because her mother, who lived on the Air Force Base, had just been stationed to Hawaii. It was a little foggy out and the first time I had ever driven in the cold, but the roads seemed okay.

We were running a little late that morning and I was slightly stressed, and there was frost on the grass but I didn't see any snow, so I wasn't too worried. I like to drive in the right lane on my way to school because I only have to make a right turn. Taylor and I were chatting, I was still keeping my eyes on the road though, but everyone else was driving about twenty miles an hour, which I didn't understand, since the speed limit was seventy. I knew that it was cold and remembered my driver's ed teachers saying that even when there isn't snow on the ground, if you saw frost you had better go slower than usual, but they never said how slow, so I figured fifty or fifty-five would do it. Because I was getting slightly annoyed I decided to pass the van in front of us. But as I reentered the right lane we began to spin off the road, we thought I hit black ice which a few cars had already done that morning."

"As we spun things became sort of a blur, sort of like I just was reacting without thinking. All I can really remember doing was what they had told us to do in drivers ed. I guess it was a subconscious thing. The irony was that I used to mock the fact we were forced to take that class! As we spun off the road I heard a noise that sounded like my back end was hitting something, and the only other noise I heard was Taylor yelling at me to make it stop.

When we finally did come to a stop we found ourselves in one of the ditches that was filled with water. The ditch was full of cattail and tall grass. The front of the car was facing the road. Taylor and I just sat there in stunned silence at what had just happened and neither of us was sure what to do.

"I asked Taylor if she was okay, and besides being on edge, she was fine. We weren't sure how far in we were, if the car would flood if we got out or not. Neither of us had any idea what to do. We figured we were deep enough we couldn't drive out and didn't want to risk it. Later, I found out that if we had gone an inch or two further we would have flooded the car when we opened the doors.

"So we both called our moms on our cell phones. Her mom was on active duty and mine was a nurse, so sadly neither of our mothers answered, so we left voice mails. My dad was in Missouri on business for the military, which always seems to be the case when something like this happens in military families.

"When we left our voice mails for our moms, we were crying so much they could only make out the words: 'spun off the road' and 'water.' So we found out later that when our moms heard this they went into a panic because of the fact that they instantly thought of the bridge that we had to cross to get over the river to school.

"We were still jittery and unsure of what to do, I was trying to remember what they told us in class during those situations, sadly they never told us exactly what to do if you landed in a water-filled ditch. Should we stay or get out? Should we turn the car off? We were unsure of the answers.

"After what felt like a half an hour, in actuality it was probably just five minutes, a red ford truck pulled over. A man with a short military hair cut got out of the truck, walked over to us, and asked if we were okay and what had happened. We told him everything that we had just gone through. He told us that he had heard of a few other cars that had the same problem and that the tow trucks were very busy and having a hard time.

"Normally, I wouldn't tell a complete stranger all that stuff, but he seemed okay. When we told him that we had called our moms but hadn't heard back he offered to let us sit in his car where it was warm, re-call our moms, and wait for them to come.

"We had no desire to sit in the car alone so without even giving it too much thought we grabbed our bags and got into his truck. The icy water soaked through my shoes and into my socks as I got out of the car and stepped into the water.

"We called our moms again, no answer. I told the guy I thought I hit something but he couldn't figure out what. He said that he might be able to pull my car out, but didn't want to risk damaging it and it was too deep in. I was upset, afraid that they would take away my license, and that my parents would be upset and started crying again. The man was clearly not used to a hysterical teenaged girl in his truck, let alone two, tried to comfort us, though Taylor had stopped crying and was also trying to comfort me. He told me that at least no one was hurt, I didn't hit any other cars, and that the state wouldn't take my license away.

"That was when my mom called and she couldn't understand me because I was still crying, so the guy offered to talk to her. He told her where we were, that we were okay, how I might have hit something, and everything else. He sat there with us till my mom showed up and then stayed another half an hour for Taylor's mom to show up. We later found out I had hit a road marker and he mentioned that if the sign that flashed the road conditions, which hadn't been put up for winter yet, if it had been there we would have flipped over completely.

"I never got his name, I don't know if he was going to work or what. But he was really nice. When I tell this story to my friends who don't live in North Dakota they ask what was I thinking getting into the truck of some stranger off the highway, wasn't I scared he would try to hurt me or something? I just shrug because after that I realized it had been what I had come to expect from people in North Dakota, people who helped you without anything in return or without a second thought."

Slowly, we all came back to the semicircle. We saw a tear in Leah's eye, which she quickly wiped away.

21.

Mayville Hitchhiker

You don't need your thumb when it's cold.
Just keep your hands in your pockets, your face under your hoodie
and stay crouched over as you walk along the road.
Anywhere else, they'd think you had bad written all over you.
But here, people understand.

"My name is Estevan Carillo," said the mischevious looking kid sitting next to Leah, with a sly, but slightly suppressed smile. "And my story is about one night when I got really hungry and decided to go to the store."

The three other Hispanic kids started to chuckle under their breath. I was starting to guess that these were the same four kids David Fuerte had talked about in his story, all friends up from San Diego.

"Yeah, he's crazy, man," said the shortest of the Hispanic guys, whose story we hadn't heard yet. This time, it wasn't just the Hispanic kids laughing. Much of the whole class chuckled.

"Okay," Estevan started in again, "the name of my story is 'If You're Out There, Help Me' – "

"Yeah, you need some help, man," the shorter Hispanic chimed in again, causing another ripple of chuckles to pass through the semicircle. This time, Dr. Baker furrowed her brow and the chuckling quickly stopped.

"Okay, it was on February twenty-seventh," Estevan said, "and it was snowing. But I had a very vital mission and that was to get to Cenex from my dorm, because I was *really* hungry. At first no one wanted to go with me and thought I was crazy, because it was really cold and none of us had a car or even ever really gotten any good winter clothes and the Cenex was a mile away and there is hardly nobody out at ten, but I was really hungry and thirsty. So, I decided to go on my own. I *visioned* myself in the television show 'Man versus Wild.'

"The temperature was below zero, the snow was up to my knees, and I was struggling just to lift one foot after the other. As the wind carried little shards of snow all around me, it drove tiny pieces of snow into my face even though I had the ties on my hoodie tightened all the way. As I left the dorm, I saw no one in sight and I thought 'Why would anybody be outside at this time?'"

"Yeah, *why?*" I heard whispered from somewhere.

Little chuckles rippling again, quietly. "*Craaaazy...*" whispered from somewhere.

I could tell Estevan was loving this moment by the twinkle in his eyes. He was clearly in his element, entertaining people by telling them about some adventure he'd undertaken outside the box of normal caution.

"Pretty soon, I noticed headlights shining behind me. I looked around as I kept walking, it was a small hatchback style with no one inside but the driver. He had driven by me, but then stopped and rolled down his window.

"He said, 'Hey, kind of cold out here tonight, huh?' with a grin on his face.

"I said, 'Yeah, a little,' hoping he wouldn't just have rolled by just to be funny and leave me, but then he laughed and asked,

"'Where are you going?' and I told him to the Cenex and he offered me a ride.

I accepted, obviously, but when I got inside I started to smell a strange odor. I turned my head and started to laugh as three giant trash bags were lying in the back seat. Maybe he was heading to the dump?

Little noises of amusement rippled around the semicircle.

"Then it was completely dark but only the little light from the gauges on his dash board. I noticed my hands were getting sweaty. Then I realized his car must have had an amazing heater, because this man looked like he had taken a shower, and it did not bother him one bit. As we reached Cenex, I didn't even bother asking him his name, but I did say, 'Thank you for your kindness, I really appreciate it.' Then I bolted out the car door. It was too hot and stinky in there!

"I watched him drive away and stood in the snow storm, which didn't feel as cold because I felt like I had been in a stinky Jacuzzi..."

All-out laughter at that one. Even Dr. Baker was laughing.

"I went into the Cenex. I picked up six Power Aides, four Roma's pizzas, and a jar of grape jelly, all for about ten dollars. After I finished paying, I walked out the door and a gust of wind and snow blew me backwards. I said to myself, 'I think I'm gonna wait for a while to see if the weather calms down.'"

"After about twenty minutes or so, I was ready to restart my journey back to the dorms. After I started walking down the road with my stuff, about six cars passed me. Then a lucky number seven car stopped ahead of me and offered me a ride. I gladly accepted, and in my mind I thought to myself how lucky I had been to get a ride to Cenex and then another one back to my dorm.

"And luckily this man's car was clean, no bizarre odor, and the heater was just warm, not a *griller*. I struck up a conversation with him and learned his name was John. I never learned his last name. John was a middle-aged man with a big family. He drove a minivan. We talked about how the people where I'm from in California wouldn't really give other people rides in a crazy storm.

"'Jolly John' I called him. He came to wrap up my night with a fun and enjoyable time down the streets of Mayville.

"Those two men have given me a whole new meaning of what a good person can be inside themselves, even though one was weird and stinky, they made me realize that there are people in this world that are willing to help others, and these kinds of people are here in North Dakota, my new home."

That last made me wonder if Estevan was planning to stick around after he graduates. I kind of doubt it – too much of an adventurer right now. But it wouldn't surprise me if he comes back later, like a lot of folks who've been here at one time or another eventually do.

22.

The Kind Viking

Two McDoubles with cheese and a side of Anonymous Kindness.

Dr. Baker didn't have to say anything. The short kid with "plug" type earrings and a goatee sitting to Samuel's left started in all by himself.

"My name is Edsel, and Estevan, Jordan and David and I went to West Acres Mall in Fargo in the winter when it was snowing. We went shopping in all kinds of stores, and after three hours we were starting to get really hungry. It started to get dark so we left the mall around seven-thirty. We began driving around so we could have some options on where to eat.

"Estevan wanted to go to McDonalds, so we all agreed. When we got there, the boys began to order. As they were ordering, a big man with a long beard walked through the door and stood behind me. He looked very extraordinary. He reminded me of a Viking, except he had big huge boots, a camouflage jacket with a matching hat. As I was trying to see what I wanted, his breathing grew a bit loud and bothersome. I was trying so hard to focus on ordering my food rather than his breathing being so loud. Soon the lady at the register saw me and said, 'Next in line, please.'

"I ordered two McDoubles with cheese and a large coke with a large order of fries. I had left my debit card in Mayville. I only had cash on me, enough to buy some things I needed at the mall, but now I noticed that I did not have enough for my order! It was almost six dollars and I only had four. I'm like frantically searching my other pockets to see what else I had, and I realized I had nothing, just the four dollars!

"As soon as I was going to tell the lady I didn't have enough money, the 'Viking' behind me tapped my shoulder. He just handed me a couple of dollar bills to complete my order. I was stunned. I didn't know what to say. I just said "thank you" with a huge smile. I didn't think anyone would give me a couple dollar bills to complete my order, especially someone like him.

"I sat down with the boys to eat our food and I told them about it, but they didn't believe me. So after we finished our food, I walked up to the man who had given me a couple of dollars, 'cause he was still there eating, and I said, 'Thank you so much for the money, but you didn't have to. I really appreciate it.'

"And he said 'No problem, have a nice day.' And then my friends believed me, because I wouldn't just walk up to a random person and say that and have them say that back to me.

After we got back on the road and headed back to the 'Ville,' which is what I call Mayville, we started calling the guy the 'Kind Viking.'"

23.

A Brit in Mayville

"I went home to my little town in England over the summer, and the first few days I kept saying 'hi' to people on the street like we do here. They just kept looking at me like I was crazy. I finally remembered to quit doing it."

We were down to the second-to-last person in Dr. Baker's semicircle. "Alright Adam," Dr, Baker said to him, "Please tell Marc about your experiences here."

"My name is Adam Edwards," he began, his voice and manner immediately striking me as a modern, red-headed version of the classic British movie star Errol Flynn, "I am originally from a small village just outside London, England. I have lived away from home since I was seventeen, and the people here in Mayville are so kind and caring, it has really helped me feel comfortable away from home.

"When I first arrived, I was invited to the house of Gwen Shaffer and Stan Dakken, during the summer of 2010, along with the Mayville State Head Coach Justin Johnson. I had come to Mayville on a recruiting trip for basketball, to experience the college before I attended in the fall. On that first occasion, we sat and talked about Mayville and its history. Gwen was born in Mayville, but had moved around the U.S. during her life. She returned in 2001 to look after Stan. Stan has lived in Mayville all his life, and has been going to every single basketball game since he was six years old! Stan is now seventy-five.

"I had to fly back to England after that to get everything in order.

"The next time I saw Gwen and Stan, it was the middle of the pre-season with Mayville State Men's Basketball team, and I was practicing to play my first game for the team. I had joined the team two weeks late as I had to wait for my VISA. Through one of the doors entered Gwen and Stan and two other individuals to come and watch us practice. Everyone began to introduce themselves, and the first thing Gwen asked, even without me saying my name, was 'How was your flight? Have you got everything you need?'

"This shocked me at first. Gwen, who had only met me once before, was asking these questions to make sure I was okay. This was my first experience of the many kindnesses that Gwen, Stan and others were to show me.

"Soon, it was the beginning of the season, the first home game of the year, and I was extremely nervous. There were a lot of expectations placed upon me. England isn't known for its basketball, so having an English player at Mayville State had some uncertainty surrounding it. I was in the locker room, getting ready to play my first official game as a Mayville Comet, visualizing the game and the different scenarios that might occur. Once I had finished visualizing, I got dressed and walked through the doors into the main gymnasium, and there sat Gwen! She saw me walk past, put her hand up and ushered me towards her. I sat down beside Gwen and asked her how things were and what she had been up to. Gwen graciously asked me the same questions. She really helped calm me down, and that first game went very well.

"Now, ever since that first game, before every home game I always sit down with Gwen. I give her a hug, and have a nice conversation about what we have both been up to. This has become a ritual and has not been broken in the two years since I first arrived.

"After the game, once we receive our post-game speech from Coach Johnson, then shower and pack our bags to leave, we all walk into the main gymnasium to thank friends and family for attending the game. Still sitting on the bleachers from the game sits my Mayville family, Gwen and Stan. I lean over and give Gwen a hug and Stan a firm handshake. We sit down and talk about how the game went. Stan is a little bit of a comedian, always having something comical to say, you know, like 'Good game, but you would have done better if I were coaching.' Gwen acts like a mother to me, asking how I am feeling, if I thought I did well, that kind of thing.

"Gwen and Stan have become family for me here in Mayville. Having people like Gwen and Stan who care about me is really humbling. Both Gwen and Stan exemplify the kindness and caring that people in North Dakota have. For instance, if I were to walk down a street in Mayville and see an individual walking towards me I would say "Hello." And they would reply back the same. But if I were to do the same thing in London, or many other towns and cities in England, people would stop and stare at me and question what my intentions were. This actually happened to me in the summer after my freshman year at Mayville. I went home to my little town in England over the summer, and the first few days I kept saying 'hi' to people on the street like we do here. They just kept looking at me like I was crazy. I finally remembered to quit doing it. I had clearly adapted to the North Dakotan environment and mannerisms.

"I will never forget Gwen or Stan. Their kindness and humility have imprinted themselves on me – as has almost every other North Dakotan or Mayville citizen I have come across."

24.

Unexpected Buyers

"I still can't believe what that family did for me."

"Alright, Jordan," Dr. Baker said to the big guy – six-foot, two hundred and fifty pounds, I'd guess – at the far end of her class semicircle. "Why don't you finish us off?"

"Well, my name's Jordan Melendo," he started off a bit haltingly, slightly shy. "I came to Mayville State to play football from San Diego with my friends, who have already told their stories.

"My story all started in my dorm room just two weeks ago. I woke up early for a Saturday, at about eight a.m., and I was starving. My roommate, Estevan Carrillo and I always have food or something to eat in the dorm. This time we did not have a single thing to eat.

"Stunned, I told Estevan that we needed to go grocery shopping as soon as possible. Estevan nodded his head as he was getting out of bed. We soon asked one of our friends to take us to WalMart. He happily agreed because he also needed to stock up.

"When we arrived at WalMart in Grand Forks, we went into the store and stocked up on food. We walked from aisle to aisle searching for cheap, hearty food such as soup, bread, lunch meat, etcetera. We were in line to pay for our groceries when we realized Estevan had forgotten his wallet back at the dorm. I told him I would pay for the groceries.

"The cashier rang us up. The total was very close to a hundred and twenty dollars. I reached into my pocket to pull out my wallet. I got my card out, swiped it, and typed in my pin number.

"But the card was *denied!*

"I started panicking immediately. I tried to swipe it again.

"No luck.

"I asked the cashier if she could put my things aside while I called my bank. The woman looked at me with a disappointed look on her face and said, 'I'm sorry. I can't have groceries out by the cash register like this. I have to call someone to put them back.'

There was a family with two children behind us, and I didn't want to make them wait for me. So I gladly agreed with the cashier. As I was leaving to make the phone call, I apologized to the family for making them wait for a few extra minutes. The man, whom I assume was the father and husband, looked at me and said with a smile on his face, 'No worries, we're in no real rush.'

"'Thank you,' I replied with a smile of my own.

"I walked outside to make the phone call. I found out my bank had put a stop on my card because I had left California, and I was able to get it restored. I went back into the store thinking I would now have to look for groceries all over again, but the cashier that helped me before told me that my groceries were already in bags and pointed at them in a cart. I was confused, but I gave her my card so she could charge me for them.

"Then she said, 'You don't have to pay.'

"I was even more confused. She saw the confusion on my face.

"She explained, 'The family behind you in the line paid for your groceries.'

"I was in total disbelief that a stranger with whom I had never spoken in my life had just paid a hundred and twenty dollars for my groceries!

"I said to Estevan, 'Can you grab the groceries so I can thank the family?'

"I ran outside and couldn't find them. That's when I realized and thought to myself, 'This is how people described North Dakota to me.'

"I got my groceries, then Estevan and I packed the car and drove off. I still can't believe it what that family did for me. I will never forget it."

25.

Turnaround is Fair Play

While I was experiencing Mayville, she experienced Fargo.

After the semicircle, I took a well-needed break for dinner with Dr. Baker. I was scheduled to do a reading and booksigning later, which had been promoted to the entire town of Mayville.

But I was dazed. The rat-a-tat-tat of amazing stories from her students experiencing this region for the first time had, surprisingly, thrown me. I had expected two or three such stories. Instead, her students had said, in so many words, one after the other, that coming to this region "was like landing on a different planet with a different species." My cute expression was taking on much more powerful meaning for me. I needed a breather to take it all in.

"You know, Marc," Dr, Baker was telling me over our dinner trays in the Mayville cafeteria, "I was born in Savannah Georgia, and I've taught all over the world, but ever since the first time I visited the Dakotas, this is where my heart has been. I spent a few years working toward getting a teaching job in this region, so I would be able to live my life here."

Dr. Baker is very, very wise. She doesn't let on. But she is.

After dinner, my book reading, also on the campus and arranged by Dr. Baker, was attended by a little over a hundred people. It was one of the happiest events I've ever been a part of (and in my line of work these days, I get to be part of a lot of happy events).

I drove home that evening a slightly different person than had arrived in Mayville that morning. A better person.

The next day, I received this email, from Dr. Andrea Dulski-Bucholz at Mayville State:

I was unable to attend your visit to our campus yesterday, as I had an appt. in Fargo. When Dr. Nannette Bagstad, who you met at lunch, I understand, walked by my office, she asked if I was going to go to your gathering that evening. I told her I couldn't, but since I was going to Fargo, I'd maybe bring her back a Fargoan moment. Well....here was my email to her today:

Nannette,

I was chuckling to myself yesterday after our conversation: I had told you I couldn't go to Mr. de Celle's campus visit but maybe I'd bring back a "Fargoan" moment. Well as it turned out, I *did* have one!

After my appt. I stopped by Menards. I'm in the Menards parking lot and I noticed something dripping from my car. So, I first backed out and moved the car to check what type of fluid it was. I pull back into another parking spot, get out, and walk over to check what was leaking. It was water. A Menards worker came over and checked what was on the ground and agreed it was just water. I thought I better be cautious so I popped the hood and he followed me over to the car and stuck his head under the hood. ANOTHER fellow walking by came over and said, "I can help...what's up?" (He must have been an auto guy as he was very confident.) Well, it was just condensation (even though I didn't have my air conditioner on).

Certainly a "Fargoan" moment! Too funny. I had to share this with you before I forgot.

Andi

So, it must have been karma! Dr. Bagstad (Nannette) told me to forward this to you as she thought you'd get a kick out of it!

Andi

Here's what I wrote back:

Thanks, Andrea! Good story. Reminds me of another...

A young lady named Cierra who works as a receptionist for a Fargo radio station once said to me as I was waiting to go on air, "The thing I like best about Fargo is that whenever I have a car problem all I have to do is pop the hood and stand there and right away someone is helping me."

I said, "No, Cierra, you've lived here all your life, so you don't really know what you like best about Fargo. The thing you really like best about Fargo is that wherever you are you can pop the hood and just stand there and not worry about who's going to show up."

But her core point holds, it's impossible not to get rescued around here, whether you need it or not!

Man, are we lucky or what?

Marc

Book II

The Fargo Way

Life is primarily a spiritual transaction.

1.

The Fargo Way

You won't find these lessons in your Economics 101 textbook.

We first visited Fargo twelve years ago, and our first morning in town, during my first transaction in Fargo, I ran smack into the Fargo Way. I was in a daze for a long time after that. It turned my world view of what was possible in 21ˢᵗ century America on its head. You'll read that story in a few pages.

Four years later, in 2005, we'd learned enough about Fargo to know it would be a great place for our kids, then eight and ten, to grow into young adults. So we moved.

But over the next few years, something happened that I hadn't anticipated: Fargo transformed my ideas about what makes an economy work well. Not coincidentally, I learned, the things that make for a truly resilient, vibrant economy happen to be exactly the same things that create an environment that's great for kids to grow into young adults.

Before moving here, I couldn't have imagined one relatively small, albeit pretty high-tech, *Little House on the Prairie*-type community would just carry on as usual while the economic world collapsed around it. But that's what happened four years ago. Fargo's unemployment rate topped out at 4.9 percent in 2009, when the national figure was double that.

Contrary to the widespread impression around the country, Fargo's economic success has almost nothing to do with the North Dakota oil boom. That's 300 miles away, on the other side of the state, controlled largely by interests out of Texas and Oklahoma and other places with a century's experience in that often slippery-slick line of business. I've checked with a half-dozen economic experts, from the Tax Commissioner of North Dakota, to the head of the Fargo-Moorhead Economic Development Council, to the leading economics columnist in the Red River Valley for the last decade, to several local economics professors who keep a close eye on our region: ***None of them think oil has had even a five percent effect on the Fargo economy, to this day.***

But I'm getting ahead of myself. That story is later.

I will, however, give you a sneak preview of what's really behind the success here. I call it *The Fargo Way*.

Remember the old Sean Connery line in *The Untouchables*?

*You wanna get Capone? Here's how you get him. He pulls a knife, you pull a gun. He sends one of yours to the hospital, you send one of his to the morgue! That's **The Chicago Way**...*

Fargo has its own version. It goes something like:

*You want to do well? Do good. You want something? Give the other guy something better. You want people to trust you with their money? Trust them with your life. Soon, winter will come, and then the floods, and you'll be trusting total strangers with your life and property and the survival of the entire community, anyway. Besides, helping others often helps you more. That's **The Fargo Way**...*

If you haven't spent much time here, that probably sounds, well, like just so much bullsh*t.

Well, let me share some stories with you, big and small, about The Fargo Way. I'll even share one about the bullsh*t, straight from the mouth of a New Yorker, after his first three days in Fargo.

Here are some Close Encounters with The Fargo Way.

2.

Go Far

Running things the Fargo Way.

My sister, Amy O'Connor, along with her beautiful family, moved to Fargo a few years ago. I try to visit about twice a year. In 2005, I came for a visit in May, right after the first Fargo Marathon. I had just run the London Marathon and Amy's husband, Tim, jokingly suggested we could run the Fargo Marathon together the following year.

I decided to hold him to it by registering him for the 2006 Fargo Marathon as his Christmas gift that year. It was a surprise. I knew I would be spending Christmas at their home in Fargo, and thought if I gave it to him for Christmas, he wouldn't be able to back out! The Fargo Marathon website also had "Fargo Marathon Training" T-shirts. I ordered a couple, intending to wrap one up as a gift for Tim, so when he opened it under the tree, I'd tell him what the real gift was and he'd have a shirt to wear while he was training! I ordered it online.

But about a week before Christmas, I received an email saying that due to unexpected delays, the T-shirts would not be available to ship before Christmas. I was really disappointed.

I arrived in Fargo from Seattle two days before Christmas. On Christmas Eve, I was at their house when there was a knock at the front door. Amy answered it, then called out to me: "Jill, there is a man here to see you." We both were rather perplexed. Who the heck knows me in Fargo? Who would be paying me a visit at my sister's house on Christmas Eve?

At the door, on Christmas Eve, was Mark Knutson, Executive Director of the Fargo Marathon Committee! He had a gift bag filled with Fargo Marathon goodies, including a Fargo Marathon beanie cap, along with a note apologizing for not being able to deliver the T-shirt before Christmas!

I was speechless! I get teary eyed just thinking about it! It was a perfect gift for my brother-in-law and we ran the Marathon together in 2006. It was a great race, and, as always, Fargo was an amazing experience! The Northern Prairie truly is a Happy Little Planet in America!

Jill Jones, Seattle, Washington

3.

Delivered with Love

Cookies en route.

My mother, Bertha Puckering, lived to the age of 101 and passed away in April of 2003. The last three years of her life were happily spent at Elim Nursing Home, where she was well cared for – except for a sweet tooth that was best served with a cookie snack. I was living on the West Coast at the time, and during my infrequent visits, I would provide her with cookies and sweets that she quickly and generously shared with others – and so, they were thus soon depleted!

On one such visit, I noticed that Mrs. Fields Cookies, located in West Acres Mall, not far from the nursing home, had a bag of a 144 small cookies, an amount that would last my mother for several weeks, for her own pleasure as well as limited sharing. When I inquired if they ever delivered, I was informed that it was not their normal practice, but was then asked "What do you have in mind?"

After explaining my mother's need and her location, the store owner said, "Elim's not much out of my way as I drive home. I would be pleased to deliver the cookies to your mother for you once a month."

"Oh, that would be great," I said. "How much will the delivery charge be?"

"Oh, we won't charge you anything – it's not out of my way!"

Thus my mother received an abundance of cookies each month for a period of several years! Once a month my credit card would show only the cost of the cookies!

Now that's a very Fargo cookie lady!

Doug Puckering, Ferndale, Washington

4.

My First Fargo Transaction

Having a spiritual experience at a gas station.

*This was my first glimpse of how strange, new and different the Fargo Way of business was compared to any place I'd ever known. I wrote about it in **How Fargo of You,** from the view of a novice. Here's a slightly more experienced view, from a serious student of The Fargo Way.*

It happened the first morning of our first visit. At a gas station. I had to pump before I could pay. Something I'd never imagined was even possible in a high-tech metropolis – albeit a fairly small one – in 21st century America.

I couldn't find a card reader on the gas pump. It was the summer of 2001, and in Phoenix, where we lived, there'd been card readers on pumps for years. So I started looking all over. *Maybe they just put their card readers in a different place up here,* I thought.

This wasn't some little old gas station in the middle of nowhere. It was a big, modern gas station/truck stop, right off the Interstate in what seemed like the middle of Fargo, with a huge sign visible from the Interstate: **Petro**.

I looked around the side of the pump. Nothing there. Then around the back of the pump. *Oh, that's another pump, of course… which doesn't have a card reader either.* I returned to my side of the pump and looked lower. *Normal.* Then higher.

Oh. There was a sign: PLEASE PAY INSIDE.

Hmmm. I have to walk inside to pay. How quaint.

I walked toward the front doors of the truck stop. *Why don't they have card readers in Fargo yet? It's not like it's a different country or something.*

Little did I know. It was a different planet. Hidden right out in the open. I was about to get my first glimpse of what I would soon come to call *Opposite World*.

As I walked inside, I immediately noticed a perky twenty-something to my right, standing over a console with buttons and lights curving around her in a half-circle, about waist high. She looked like a sound engineer standing behind a large set of mixing boards. There were several people in a line leading up to this arrangement. She was taking their money and credit cards and pushing buttons on the console. I'd never seen anything quite like it before. I got in line.

About a minute later, I handed her my credit card. "I need to fill up on pump ten," I said.

She looked down at her console, holding my credit card aloft. Her brow furrowed. "Did you say pump ten?" she asked.

"Yeah," I said. I could tell she was puzzled by something. I had no idea what it could be.

Then came the words: "But you haven't pumped yet."

I suddenly felt myself being lifted, slowly, out of the ordinary world I'd known all my life. Images from my previous four decades started flashing by. When had anything like this ever happened to me? Nothing... nowhere... *never*...

I felt disoriented, almost dizzy. "You mean you want me to fill up... and *then* pay you?" It sounded silly as I asked it. *I must have misunderstood her. That can't be what she meant.*

A smile spread across twenty-something's face as she handed my card back to me, unused. A sparkle lit her eyes. She was quietly, but clearly, delighted. Her eyes were saying something. I could almost hear it: *Oh, good, we've got a newbie....*

Smiling broadly, she almost sang her next lines, as if she were in a Rogers and Hammerstein musical: "Yeah, that's right, just go fill up and then come baaa--ck and we'll take caaa---re of you!"

Dazed, I took my credit card back from her. I couldn't remember a previous time in my adult life when a business I'd never walked into before just assumed I was a decent person. I'd been conditioned for decades to expect to be treated as untrustworthy, as though I were a criminal, and therefore, I had to pay before getting anything, thank you very much. I still can't remember anything like this happening to me prior to that moment, not in all the decades I'd spent living in Arizona, California and Florida.

Pay before you pump was all I'd ever known. Now, suddenly, I was being told *pump before you pay*. I was entering *Opposite World* – just the barest, first glimpse of a world I hadn't imagined possible in 21st century America.

In a daze, I shuffled back out to the pump.

As the pump started clicking happily along, the hair on the back of my neck slowly stood on end. *So this is what community feels like,* I remember realizing. And I remember realizing why they didn't have card readers yet: *They don't need them!* [2]

---

[2] Almost all the gas pumps in Fargo now have card readers – they just make pumping your own gas so much easier. But they also make doing business the old way a lot harder. Think about it: When you always had to go inside to pay, it was much harder to make the mental mistake of accidentally driving off without paying. If you hadn't gone inside, you hadn't paid. Not now! If a pump with a card reader works regardless of whether you've swiped your card through it, It's much easier to absent-mindedly drive off without paying! Nevertheless, a surprising number of gas stations in town still insist on letting people pump before they pay. I tell a funny story about this in Book IV, *True Fargo Crime*.

I've spent a lot of the last twelve years trying to find out why. I'm still trying. But one thing I've come to believe: When everyone treats everyone else as if they're unworthy of trust – like they did in the world of California, Arizona and Florida, where I spent my first fifty years – it makes it much easier for most of us to behave in an untrustworthy way. Not lending your customers, on whom you depend for survival, even a modicum of trust is actually pretty stingy. The tone is thus set. Everyone out for themselves. Take what you can when the opportunity arises.

But when you anonymously extend your trust to people, it raises the expectation level everyone you come into contact with. It raises your expectations of yourself and those around you, and the cultural expectation level as a whole. It does this because it's a generous way to treat people. It's kindness in action. When enough people and businesses do it, that feeling of generosity and kindness spreads through the whole community. This sets a powerful tone. It feels good to be trusted; you tend to like a person or business that trusts you. It creates a desire not to disappoint the people trusting you.

I actually think it's a spiritual judgment. It's a business saying, "Your certainty that I trust you is more important than my certainty that I get paid for what I give you." Judgments like that have powerful reverberations, when acted upon.

And so do the opposite kinds of judgments.

I began to get a glimmer of this, and a lot of other things, during that first transaction in Fargo. It was the first spiritual experience I'd ever had at a gas station. And it was just the blade of grass growing out of the clump of dirt sitting atop the tip of the iceberg.

Marc de Celle

5.

From the Ground Up

Building on a foundation of trust.

I lived in Illinois and the San Francisco Bay area as a child, and Wisconsin and Michigan as an adult. Then, almost two years ago, we moved to Fargo, and it's been one amazing thing after another. I've started calling these "Fargo Moments."

Many people ask us why we moved to Fargo. I think this is because most people here are from North Dakota or western Minnesota, and they know about Fargo – but they also know that people in other parts of the country don't have any idea what it's like here. We had heard it was nice, but until we moved, we had no idea how different it would be.

My husband works at the Venteran's Administration (VA) hospital. He used to work at the one in Madison, Wisconsin, but then, about two years ago, he met a very nice executive from the Fargo VA at a national VA function. They hit it off, and that man, who is now my husband's boss, told him about an opening at the Fargo VA. My husband applied, got the job and we came!

Our first Fargo experience came when we built a house. I found the builder on the Internet – Titan Homes. I soon began a correspondence with Angie, the builder and owner. She was so nice I could not believe it! Not only did she personally help with everything, she accepted just $10K down for the house, and agreed to take the rest... AT CLOSING! Everyone else I've ever known who built a house had to take out huge construction loans and pay as the house was built (the basement, you pay x dollars, framing up, x dollars, roof goes on, x more dollars, bathrooms and plumbing, x dollars and so on). It made everything so much simpler this way, giving us time to sell our house in Madison and take care of all the other things we needed to take care of. What was most impressive was that Angie trusted complete strangers to actually pay for this custom house that no one else would want if she was stuck with it!

She was great throughout the entire process. One time, for instance, I changed my mind about the knobs going on the cupboards. She immediately asked if I would like her to meet me at the cabinet shop to pick out new knobs – and the cabinet maker was over a half hour from her office! That's just one of the many "Fargo moments" we had with Angie helping us move into our new, wonderful, Fargo community.

Frances Weintraub, happily ensconced in Fargo

6.

The Doctor Is Out

A Fargo kind of house call.

Before I had to start using a third leg (my cane), my husband Ed and I used to do a lot of walking. We walked to the bank, to Sons of Norway (a downtown Norwegian restaurant), the Medicine Shoppe, church, and so on. One very windy, dusty day (as North Dakota sometimes has), we walked to the Dakota Clinic. My husband had an appointment with a Dr. Brunelle, who has since retired. But he was a very Fargo doctor, as you shall see.

During the walk to the clinic, the dust had made me start to cough and sneeze, and my asthma kicked in. I joined my husband in the patient room, as I always do, and when Dr. Brunelle saw me, he mildly scolded me for being out in the dust.

Once he finished with my husband, he told us to go to the front door. A minute or two later, he pulled up to the front door in his own car! Then he told us to get in, asked our address, and drove us home, suggesting that we stay inside for the rest of the day!

How Fargo was that?

Gladys Brewer, Fargo

8.

The Not-So Chain Store Employee

Hello! This is Fargo's Club. We come to you.

This story happened about five years ago, but I continue to find it amusing. I was working on my computer to make one of those "Kodak Memory Books" for a neighbor's graduation gift. It was the first one I'd ever tried to make, and I was running into a lot of problems. I had no idea who to ask for assistance.... I believe I was trying to upload pictures to a website, as I recall. Anyway, I ended up phoning Sam's Club, simply because I didn't know who else to call, and I had purchased a camera there recently.

The man on the other end of the line, in the Photo Center, patiently tried to help me. Still no luck. Finally, he said, "Since I am about done with work, why don't I just come over to see if I can help?" Normally, I would have said no. But I was desperate. I needed to get the book completed. So I accepted his offer.

He showed up, just like he promised, after work. The funny part is, while he was helping, I kept telling him to feel free to leave at *any time*. Finally, after what I remember as quite a long while, he was able to get what I needed done and said, "Well, I guess I should get going, since it's my wife's birthday and we're going out to supper."

He tried to refuse any payment for coming over and spending his own time helping a stranger on his wife's birthday! Hopefully, his wife is also from Fargo, and so understood, and forgave him for being late!!!

Jodi Gramlow, Fargo

9.

Quit Fargoing Me Up!

North Dakota haggling.

Brian Johnson is one of our friends and neighbors. He and his lovely wife, Becky, live on a farm between Hunter and Arthur, North Dakota, about 25 miles northwest of Fargo, as the crow flies. Brian is truly one of the most generous folks we know.

Brian often tells the story of the corn harvest of 2008. It was a long, drawn out, miserable harvest, and Brian was in need of extra trucking help. He asked one of his neighbors, Steve Porter, to help him. There wasn't any talk of money. Steve quickly agreed, and assisted Brian for a couple of days. His work really eased the pressure of moving the corn to market.

A few days after the harvest, Brian met with Steve to "settle up." After he asked what he owed him, Steve gave Brian a price, but Brian felt it was much too low. Brian then negotiated the price up! And Steve didn't make it very easy, he said!

I guess that's what you call a Fargo negotiation.

Randy and Bridgette Readel, Hunter, North Dakota

10.

The Missing Stories

Keeping good deeds secret.

There are a lot of examples of the Fargo Way I can't tell you about. The businesspeople involved don't want them known.

This kind of anonymity for good deeds is endemic around here – a central feature of *Opposite World*. Opposite, at least, from where I spent my first fifty years, where it was much more typical to see people scrambling around to take credit for every possible good deed in sight, then promote it, regardless of veracity.

You'll see people eschewing credit for good deeds well done in a number of stories here. I've come to believe this plays a very central role in The Fargo Way. I'll be telling you more about why I think this is so as we go along.

You may have already noticed that none of these stories are told by the people who did the good deeds, and in most cases, I haven't asked the do-gooders for their permission to pass on the stories concerning them. I'm afraid I'd get too many refusals if I asked the actual people and companies responsible for the good deeds.

But before we move on, there's one story I can't tell you. It's a story about what we were just talking about – not wanting attention or credit for good deeds well done.

If I don't tell you the name of the company, though, I'll be forgiven. You'll see what I mean.

About a year ago, the president of a company located in the Red River Valley, which encompasses both Fargo and Grand Forks, told me that not only was every employee getting an unprecedented $2,000 Christmas bonus, but each and every employee was also being given a voucher for $1,000 to donate to the charity of their choice.

"Wow, Fred (not his real name)!" I said over the phone. "What a great thing to do! And what a great story! I know that WDAY TV would love to do a story about that! I could put you in touch with Kirsten Kealy, the co-anchor. She'd love that story! It's a great Christmas story!"

"Well..." Fred hesitated. I knew I had him, appealing to how much Kirsten would like it and that it would add so much to the local Christmas spirit. "I'm not sure..."

Hey, at least it wasn't a "no." I decided to press the first step: "I'll tell you what, Fred. I'll just put you in touch with Kirsten via email, and I'll tell her about the story, and you two can go from there. If you decide you don't want it aired, Kirsten won't air it. You can trust her."

"Well, okay, if she can be trusted..." came his very noncommittal response.

"You can."

I wrote an email introducing the two of them, and telling Kirsten what Fred's company was doing. Kirsten wrote back, saying how excited she was about the wonderful thing Fred's company was doing.

Then I heard nothing.

A couple of days later, I learned that Fred had decided he didn't want the story to get any attention, and of course, Kirsten had honored that request, just as I said (Note: Local newspeople do not honor requests not to report scandalous news! First of all, it's very rare and valuable! Second, it would be very unFargo to let bad guys just go one victimizing people.)

Fred told me, "We just didn't anyone thinking we were doing it for any other reason than the fact that it was just a good thing to do."

I really wanted to tell you more stories to show how The Fargo Way applies to the upper echelons of business around here as well as the lower, stories where I might actually be able to name names and pat backs.

But the people with the backs that deserve patting won't let me talk. Not a peep!

Oh. I just remembered one someone sent me that I can pass on, about a company has been bought and sold a couple of times since it happened – so no one can stop me!

11.

The Company that Bought the Company Is Doing What?

When corporate care isn't just PR BS.

This story comes from Paula Thompson, who grew up in Lisbon, North Dakota, a small town about an hour southwest of Fargo. It happened about 35 years ago, and it took place immediately after the company had been bought out. No company would ever be expected to act this way, much less one that had just changed ownership.

Except, maybe, around here.

In the winter my father, who was a sales executive with what was then called the Melroe Company – their most famous brand being Bobcat equipment – would bring home a Bobcat skid steer loader and go up and down the street clearing everyone's driveway of snow. We had plenty of it back then – way more than my mother and sisters, who still live in North Dakota, report these days.

We had a lot of elderly people on my street and he watched out for them…as did everyone else. Made sure their sidewalks and driveways were clear and always had a friendly wave or helping hand to lend. We grew up with everything we needed, and would never have had to work growing up. But in that part of the world it wasn't *if* you were going to have a summer job, it was *what* you would be doing. Work ethic? You betcha! Regardless of your financial circumstances.

Sadly, my father passed away unexpectedly back in 1976, at the young age of 49. We couldn't have the funeral in our small little Presbyterian church that held only about a hundred people. We had to move it to the biggest church in town, the Lutheran church, because hundreds of people showed up. Literally. I was 19 years old and had never really been to a funeral before. And I had no idea people brought *food* to the house when someone died. We had more people showing up with food and offers of help than I could count. The town rallied around my grieving mother and her four kids. I don't believe I'd find the kind of round-the-clock concern and help we received anywhere else

I've ever lived over the last few decades, since my work took my away from my beloved home state.

But that's not the amazing part of the story.

Around the time my father died, Melroe was purchased by Clark Equipment. They already had plans to move the corporate offices to Fargo. When they made that move, even though my father had died months earlier, the company paid to move my mother to Fargo, too, so she could be near the people who were her closest friends, my father's coworkers and their families.

Where else would you find a company with a heart like that?

Paula Thompson, Columbus, Ohio

12.

Brilliant Kindness

Laying down a good foundation with a doggie door.

In **How Fargo of You***, I told the story of the first time I hired John Skarphol, the carpenter. But there's more to the story than I told; I later realized what a brilliant way of doing business this story exemplifies.*

I'd met John at a local rock concert through our mutual friend, Melody. It was a thirty-second introduction between songs, then we went our separate ways.

A few weeks later, just after Charlene, the kids and I moved in to our new house in Fargo, we needed a doggie door. I called Melody, and got John's number from her. I called John that evening and asked if he'd be willing to take a look at it sometime for me. He told me he was building a house, but he'd come by after work the next day and take a look.

He arrived about four in the afternoon, having put in a full day's work. I was hoping to get an estimate and set up a weekend appointment or something. Instead, once I showed him the door I'd bought and where I wanted it, he just started sawing a hole in the wall! I needed that door and he knew it. I wasn't going to stop him.

It was a north wall, and it was six inches thick ("for extra insulation – that north wind is a B..."). That was a good thing, except it meant the bolts that came with the doggie door weren't long enough to put everything together. John had to custom-make bolts that were long enough using a hacksaw and threaded dowels!

He did truly excellent work, and three hours after arriving, the doggie door was beautifully in place, right where we wanted it. (John would have finished much sooner, but when I ran off to buy the threaded dowels so John could keep working, I didn't follow his instructions – I tried to find actual bolts that were the right size, even though John had told me I wouldn't.)

Anyway, as John was cleaning up, I pulled out my checkbook. I expected to pay him something over $200. He was highly skilled, he'd gone out of his way to deliver what I needed in the shortest possible time after a full day's work elsewhere, and he'd done a great job. I figured $75 an hour was the least his time had been worth.

"So John, what do I owe you?" I asked.

"Nothing, it's a housewarming gift," came the answer up from the floor, where he was crouched and picking up his tools.

I was dumbstruck. Could hardly speak.

"No, John, uhhh, you can't be… uhhh, I mean, you've been uhhh, here three hours, came after a full day's uhhh, work, did a great job…"

While I was fumbling the words out, John got up, came over and put out his hand to shake mine. With a big grin he said, "Welcome to Fargo."

That was where I left the story in *How Fargo of You*.

But there's more, and that's what I want to tell you now. Six or seven months later, after the spring thaw, Charlene and I decided to build a pool deck in our back yard, for above-ground pool.

We wanted a nice, big deck. One that would hold a lot of people. It would be a big job, and run well into the thousands of dollars.

We didn't call around for estimates. We just called John. *Of course.* And this time, he let me pay him!

You can take a cynical view of this, if you choose to. I feel sorry for you if you do. Because nothing about any of it felt the least bit jaded, at any point. John loved doing it, and I loved experiencing it.

But it wasn't the least bit dumb. It was *brilliant*.

That's the way business is expected to work around here.

And man, does it work.

Kindness is good business.   Extraordinary kindness can be brilliant business. Perhaps the most brilliant way to do business of all, for a myriad of reasons. What if it were the predominant way of doing business throughout the world?

Thanks, John, for being the first to teach me that.

Marc de Celle

13.

Retail Comforting

Treating customers like family. Seriously.

Everyone knows there is something a little bit different about our family when we are out in public. It is my eight year old son, Chandler. Most are caught off guard by his piercing blue eyes and striking features. Handsome and quiet. He doesn't speak because he has severe autism. We have gotten many comments and stares over the years, and some situations are awkward, like when strangers ask "What grade are you in?", or simply his name. If you watch him carefully, you'll see the quick movements of his fingers flipping back and forth repeatedly, or notice that he is stepping on each and every tile square on the floor. These things are far more noticeable some days than others.

I have always loved the local grocery store chain Hornbacher's for their staff diversity, employing lots of people with special needs wherever they can. But one day I learned a lesson in how special my community, and their store, is. It was a hot summer day in July 2010, and we were on a very short trip for milk that quickly turned into more than I bargained for. The crowd in the store was making Chandler anxious, and he began whimpering and hiding behind me instead of pushing the cart. When he is upset, only select aisles are acceptable for shopping, and today it was very few. We managed to take out a display of snack crackers, and a young stock boy just smiled and said, "No problems." In less than five minutes, Chandler managed to also tear open a box of Pop tarts, and a candy bar. He screamed like a fire alarm every time I took something from his hands and placed it back on the shelf. I was praying I was getting looks of empathy rather than irritation. He is much faster than I give him credit for, and while I was looking for Kleenex to wipe my tears, he suddenly had a tangerine. He sniffed it, and held it out to me to sniff too. This seemed to calm him down, so I let him hold it while we walked to the checkout. I was relieved to see a familiar cashier ready to ring us up. Because we are frequent visitors, I was a little more comfortable going as slowly as I was at emptying the cart, since I had to make sure Chandler didn't disappear or remove candy bars from the checkout display.

Then I saw the tangerines. Two in the cart, one mangled and dripping in his hand, which he again sniffed and held out to me with a smile. I began to tell the cashier I would gladly pay for them. She handed me a tissue and said, "How about ten cents?"

I think she knew allowing me to pay would alleviate some of my feelings of discomfort. My eyes couldn't stop the tears anymore. "Thank you," I said. If I could have gotten more words out, quite possibly it would have been "How Fargo of you."

Nicole Thorson, Fargo

14.

Gas Prices Just Went Down. Dramatically.

Around here, mistakes are often just another excuse to be honorable and generous.

About two months ago, as I was out running errands, I realized I needed gas in my car. I do not pump my own gas. Usually my husbands does (what a guy!) or else I go to a full service station – which for me is Bob's Oil, here in Grand Forks, North Dakota. So I pull in to Bob's and realize I only have twenty dollars cash and no checkbook!

"Can I just get twenty dollars' worth of gas?" I asked the service attendant.

"Okay," he says, pump going, and starts to wash all my windows, doing a great job! Suddenly, I look at my total on the pump, and it's moving fast! It's $15, then $18, and I quickly say out the window, "I only want twenty dollars' worth!"

But by the time he stops the pump, it reads $30.00. He apologizes for the mistake and tells me, "You only owe me twenty dollars."

"I have a credit card, and I can put it on that," I tell him.

"No, it was my mistake, I won't let you pay for more than you asked for."

What a North Dakota guy!

Elaine Fetsch, Grand Forks, North Dakota

15.

Seeing More Business in the Future

Giving is better than receiving. Even in business, in the long run.

About a month ago, the bow on my glasses broke. I waited a few weeks until I knew I had enough money to pay for a new frame. I went to the eye clinic at Essentia Health and picked out a new frame while I waited for the optometrist.

When he arrived, I first showed him my broken frame and asked, hopefully, "Can these be fixed?"

He said, "You know, I have a box of assorted bows and frames - let me see what I can find."

About ten minutes later he came back and showed me my glasses, with a new bow on them! "The bow I found isn't exactly like the original one," he said, "but is it close enough?"

"It surely is!" I said, with a big smile.

"Good! Have a nice day!" He replied.

I did not have to pay a dime. This Fargo thing has happened to me before plenty of times, because I've lived here since 1972 – but each time it does, I am left speechless!

Maybe next time, I'll say, "How Fargo of you!"

Marnie Aleckson Blatchford, Fargo

16.

Three New Yorkers Finding Fargo

"I know this is all just a f!~ing act."*

Twenty years ago, I'm told, downtown Fargo was a bit of a pit. Today it's a beautiful, bustling beehive. But don't take my word for it. Take it from a couple of New Yorkers.

About a year ago, a couple out of New York City, A.J. and Melissa Leon, decided to put together an international conference for artists, entrepreneurs and other creative types called "The Misfit Conference." But they decided not to hold it in NYC.

Turns out, they'd visited Fargo. "The amount of art and creativity per square block in Fargo completely overwhelms

New York City," A.J. told the first Misfit conference, held in downtown Fargo this last summer, with attendees from as far away as Sri Lanka, Europe and Thailand. And I noticed a minute ago, just looking at their website for the second annual Misfit Conference, that it's already sold out!

I'm using A.J. and Melissa to introduce you to Karen Stoker. Because if anyone kick-started the revitalization of downtown Fargo into high gear at the outset of the 21st century, it was Karen.

She took the Mona Lisa approach. That's what I call it. You know, you've got a mess. It's kind of a widespread, scattered mess. What do you do? Typically, most of us try to eliminate the worst parts of it until it's not quite as bad, then the next worst parts, and so on.

But then, there's also the Mona Lisa approach. You pick one spot out of the mess, claim it, and create a masterpiece. You trust your example will radicalize standards, and lots of other people will then try to create their own masterpieces, too. That's what Karen did. And it worked.

It's called the Hotel Donaldson. In the early part of the 20th century, it was the centerpiece of Fargo. But by the approach of the 21st century, Karen says, generously, "it was tired and worn."

Then Karen bought it. Lock, stock and barrel. Now it's a masterpiece. It would've been cheaper and easier to tear it down and build from scratch, but that wouldn't have been the Mona Lisa approach. Instead, Karen chose to gut and rebuild from the basement up, preserving every possible piece of the original.

Then she made each room an individual masterpiece, featuring the art of a local artist. Then "Stoker's Basement" was finished, featuring a pictorial history of the Hotel and its restoration. Finally, an open-air rooftop lounge was added, with a great view of downtown.

That was just the beginning. Today, the hotel boasts North Dakota's only four-diamond rated restaurant and just received Wine Spectator's 2013 Award of Excellence.

I first met Karen in the HoDo Lounge, on the west end of the ground floor. The music was great, the place bustling. It was a little over two years ago, not long after *How Fargo of You* had hit the town like a small tornado. Karen was sitting with Alison, who manages the hotel, and who I knew, because the hotel was already giving away copies of *How Fargo of You* to their guests. I don't remember if I'd arranged for this meeting to happen, or if it was happenstance, but I was delighted to finally meet the woman who'd kick-started the revitalization of downtown, amidst her Mona Lisa.

The place was very busy. Alison, a gracious, attractive and ridiculously competent thirtysomething woman, introduced us. Karen smiled a great smile and we shook hands. "Hi, nice to meet you," she said, moving to the empty stool to her left, offering me the stool between her and Alison.

This lady knows hospitality, I thought to myself.

"It's great to meet you, too, Karen," I said. "I've wanted to meet you for a long time. I love this place, and really admire what you've done."

"Thank you," she said. "Would you like a drink?"

"What are you having?" I asked her, looking at the yummy-looking coffee drink she had in her hand. I love coffee drinks.

"Spanish coffee," she said, drawing the words out in a way that made it sound especially delicious.

"Hmmm," I said, intrigued. "What's in it?" I asked.

"I don't know," Karen said, again kind of slowly, smiling, "I just know it's *delicious*..."

"It's got coffee in it," Alison chimed in, and we all laughed.

Karen pointed toward the bartender as he poured a drink for a patron. "He made me one a while back, and I've been having one in the evening *quite often* ever since."

The bartender came by. "I'll have one of those," I said, pointing at Karen's drink.

"Spanish coffee coming right up," he said, and went to work on it.

"I love coming here," I said to Karen. "It's really amazing what you've created" – I turned to Alison – "and how well it runs."

My Spanish coffee arrived, almost instantly. I started to get my wallet out, but Karen immediately put up her hand to stop me: "It's on us."

This lady knows hospitality.

"Well, this place has been a work of love," Karen said, and Alison raised her glass in a toast. We all clinked.

I sipped. It was *insanely* great. It was far and away the best coffee drink I'd ever had. Still is. And I've had more at the HoDo since then, just to make sure.

Our conversation quickly turned to my book, and what it was like to move to Fargo as a newcomer, having never set foot on the Northern Prairie before our first visit.

"Well, if you've only lived in California and Arizona, you really don't know human beings can behave this way, en masse," I remember saying, kind of wide-eyed. "It was just one great culture shock after another. So I finally had to write about it…"

"That reminds me of this guy who came in from New York once," Karen said. "Back when we were doing Great Plains –"

Aside: Microsoft's second-largest field campus on earth is located in Fargo. That's because a little company called Great Plains Software was founded in Fargo about thirty years ago, and soon after, it came under the ownership and management of a young local guy named Doug Burgum. Karen was married to Doug, and helped build the company into a very successful business that Microsoft bought around the turn of the 21st century. Since then, Doug has been revitalizing much of the rest of downtown Fargo, along with pursuing about a dozen other ventures.

Back to our story…

"—we started having annual conventions," Karen explained, "where we'd fly people in from all around the world, usually our most successful salespeople, and we'd put them up for a three-day event. And one year, one of the salespeople we flew in was from New York City. I'm not sure he'd ever been away from the East Coast before. And at the end of the first afternoon, when people were leaving the seminar room because it was time for dinner, he came up to me at the front of the room and said, sort of under his breath, 'I just want you to know that I know that this is all just a f*!~ing act.' And I was a little surprised, but I just smiled and asked, 'Yeah?' to draw him out a little, and he said, 'I know this is bullsh*t, I just want you to know, *I know you people aren't really this way.*' And then I got it, and I chuckled a little, I didn't want to laugh too hard right then, but I knew what he was saying, and I just patted him on the back and said, 'Okay, that's fine, thanks for telling me.' Later that night, of course, I shared it with some of the staff and we just *howled!*"

Alison and I were howling too, at this point.

"But that's not the best part. A couple of days later, I was arranging everyone's transportation to the airport, and he came down the stairs of the hotel, and he came up to me kind of sheepishly, and he said, 'I just want to apologize to you for what I said that first day I was here.'

"And I said, 'No, that's fine, I understand, don't worry about it,' but he said, 'No, really, now I realize: *You people really are this way!*' and there was a tear running down his cheek! And I gave him a big hug and thanked him…"

142

"He had a tear running down his cheek?" I asked, loudly.

"Yeah! He'd had a real culture shock, but a great one, just like the ones you wrote about that you kept having!"

"Well, I've had a lot of tears rolling down my cheeks these last six years, since we moved here, for just the same kinds of reasons…"

Marc de Celle

17.

Bus Service

Anyone who's ever ridden a bus or a train knows that mass transit often hits a snag. Around Fargo, though, this can lead you on a surprise journey.

I grew up near Fargo, in Glyndon, Minnesota. But, like many others, I moved away for college and stayed away for seventeen years. In 1994 I moved back (only temporarily, I thought!) to take a couple of classes at Minnesota State University in Moorhead (known locally as MSUM), just across the Red River from Fargo. I also got a part-time job and, since I didn't have a car at the time, my brother would drive me to campus in the morning. After class, I'd take the bus to my job in north Fargo.

One day my bus got caught waiting for a train in Moorhead. This wasn't unusual, and whenever it happened, the driver would radio ahead to the Fargo station and have them hold any buses he had transfers for. This time, however, there was a miscommunication, and when we arrived at the Fargo station, my bus had already left! So I asked the dispatcher what time the next bus for my route would leave.

"One o'clock," he told me.

"I'm supposed to be at work at one o'clock," I sighed, "but I guess there's no help for it."

"Where do you work?" the dispatcher asked.

I told him the address.

"If you can hang on just a couple of minutes," he told me, "I get off at twelve-thirty, and I'll drive you up there in the company car."

I got to work on time that day, thanks to a dispatcher who went way beyond the call of duty to help a customer. And I chuckled to myself all the way because I'd spent the previous 17 years in Chicago, Houston, and Vienna, and there was no way in heck I'd have gotten into a car with a stranger in any of those cities, no matter how nice they seemed or how dire my situation was. But hey--this is Fargo!

Lorelee Benz, Fargo

18.

"No Problem"

Kids these days. "No problem" this and "no problem" that.

I have a story to tell you that just happened to me about an hour ago. Talk about a "How Fargo of You" moment!

I've been busy doing Christmas baking for the past week and wanted to get some baked goods in the mail today, using the flat rate boxes from the post office, as I've done in the past.

So I got up early this morning and drove over to the local Hornbacher's Grocery store to find out the latest I'd be able to bring a package into the store and still catch the mailman. The cashier told me the mailman picked the mail up about 4:00 pm, but suggested that with the Christmas rush, I had better get it there at least an hour early.

It was 7:30 am. I went home and packed two boxes of homemade goodies; kuchen, banana bread, zucchini bread, peanut butter balls, almond joys, melting moments, soda cracker bars, orange cookies, salted nut rolls, chocolate chip cookies, a bag of GIANT sunflower seeds (from Wahpeton, North Dakota), and included a copy of your book, "How Fargo of You," all bound for Sparks, Nevada. After packing everything in bubble wrap and sealing up the boxes, I placed them into the freezer so everything would be frozen when it left North Dakota (that was my hope, anyway).

I arrived at Hornbacher's about 2:45 pm. The young man behind the service counter said I could set my boxes down on the counter by the postage scale and come around to the other side where the cash register was, which I did. He then proceeded to weigh the boxes.

Sending the boxes would cost $14.50 each, $29.00 dollars for both, he told me. Then he apologized for them costing so much!

"Do you still want to mail them?" he asked.

"Of course I do!" Then, as a joke, I added, "It would be nice if you put them in the freezer until the mailman arrives." The lady in line behind me laughed. She'd probably baked things and mailed them before herself, and got the joke!

But the young man simply said, "That's no problem, I can do that for you."

"Are you sure?"

"It's not a problem, we have a big freezer in the back."

"That's really nice of you, but will you really remember the boxes are in the freezer when the mailman comes?"

He said, "Sure I will, I'll just write myself a note."

"Well, thank you again, that's wonderful!"

As I left the store, I thought to myself, no place other than Fargo could I trust another person to remember my gifts, and no other place would something like this happen. I thought to myself, "Now that's 'How Fargo of You.'"

After I got back home, I started baking the last of the kuchens. Suddenly, from some place in my brain, it occurred to me that I had addressed the two boxes to RENO, NV, not SPARKS, NV. I was getting ready to run back to the store to change the address when I realized I couldn't leave the house, because the kuchens were in the oven and wouldn't be done baking for another 25 minutes.

"By that time," I said to myself, "The postman will have already come and gone!" So, what would a Fargo person do, but just pick up the phone and call Hornbacher's? So I did.

A young man's voice answered the phone: "Hornbacher's, this is Tylor. How may I help you?"

I said, "Tylor, are you the person behind the service counter"?

He said, "Yes, I am."

"This is Terri, and I'm the one who brought in the two boxes of baked goods you placed in the freezer."

"I remember you." I could tell by the way he said it, he was smiling. I told him about my mistake and asked if he would change the addresses on the boxes from Reno, Nevada to Sparks, Nevada.

By now, you probably know what Tylor said.

"That's no problem, I can do that for you." Then he added: "Is there anything else you need?"

I said, "No, Tylor, no thank you, you have helped me a lot! Not everyone would have done what you have!" I couldn't resist adding: "How Fargo of you!"

"What?" He had no idea what I was talking about. So I just said, "Thank you!"

"You're welcome," he said, and hung up.

I plan on going into the store on Monday morning on my way to work at 6:00 am. I want to make sure the manager knows what a GREAT employee he has. And also to let him know I've sent the story of Tylor's good deeds to you. Maybe, just maybe, Tylor and Hornbacher's may make it into "How Fargo of You, Too!" or whatever you decide to call your next book!

Terri R. Busch, Fargo (When I worked at the University of Reno in Nevada, my nickname was "Fargo"!)

Editor's note: After Terri sent me this story, I had to know how it ended, so I wrote her back. Here is her response:

I returned to Hornbacher's the next morning at 6:00 am to let the manager know of his outstanding employee. I was told the manager wasn't in at the time, but would in be later in the morning. I was able to catch up with him at noon on my way home for lunch.

The manager was pleased I was treated to outstanding service and was happy the young man had made the extra effort. I told him I was going write to you and tell my "Hornbacher's story." The manager smiled and asked me to let him know if anything became of it.

And the goodies arrived right on time in Nevada still cold – just like anything coming from Fargo for Christmas should!

19.

Lakeside Service

This kind of thing happens a lot in the summer in the lakes area of Minnesota, just east of Fargo. I've heard stories like this a dozen times. Thankfully, Jill actually wrote hers down and sent it to me!

We live on Lake Lida, in Minnesota, about fifty miles southeast of Fargo. Recently, our son, who's in his thirties and living in Fargo, brought a group of friends out to the lake. They took our pontoon out and decided to stop at Maple Beach Resort & Grill, a great place where you can just dock your boat and get the best burgers. Unfortunately, like a lot of places away from the big city, they don't take credit cards, which is all my son and his friends had with them. However, when my son explained that his parents lived on the lake and would come by later and pay the bill, they all got their burgers and fries! A few days later, I stopped to pay the bill, which came to $48. The owner remembered the situation, but had nothing in writing other than my son's word that we would pay!

How Fargo is that?

Jill Holsen, Pelican Rapids, Minnesota, in loving memory of David Holsen, loving husband and father.

20.

Heading off to Parts Known

An adventure in Fargo refrigeration.

It was the morning of Friday, December 24th, just three days ago. My wife had gone off to pick up a few extra "white elephant" gifts to share at her family's Christmas gathering up in Buxton, North Dakota, later in the evening. I went outside to clear snow from our driveway that has seen too much snow for this time of the year.

As I came back into the house I heard a "chirp" in our house. At first I thought it was one of the kids' alarms or a smoke detector. I finally figured out it was our refrigerator. Having a somewhat "modern" fridge, it has an alarm on it letting you know when something is wrong! How great is that? Before all our food spoiled and ice melted onto our floor our fridge had actually let us know that something bad was going to happen.

We proceeded to take all of our refrigerated food out to our garage, which, in the Fargo winter, doubles as an enormous walk-in refrigerator. We organized the stuff on my long workbench. We then took all our frozen items, put them in a plastic tub and placed it in the world's largest walk-in freezer, the great North Dakota outdoors. This whole process delayed us less than an hour, and just before noon we were off to the Christmas Eve gathering with my wife's family in Buxton.

The next day, Christmas, I was thinking about who to call to get the refrigerator fixed. I decided to look some information up on the Internet. I found a couple of great resources that described in detail how to go about troubleshooting the problem, and was able to quickly diagnose what the problem was. It appeared the refrigerator just needed one part replaced. The next chance I would have to get that part would be Sunday at noon, when stores would open back up again.

Noon sharp, I was the first person in the doors of NODAK appliance, Sunday, the day after Christmas. I asked them if they had the part. The Parts department was closed, of course, but one of the appliance salespeople said, while he wasn't very good with the Parts department computers, he would do what he could. He looked up the part number, as well as a replacement part number, but found they did not stock either.

Now I had to wait until Monday to see if anyone in the Fargo area had the part I was looking for. All the while, our wonderful climate was keeping our food either nicely chilled, in the garage, or frozen solid, right outside.

My first call Monday morning for my part did not yield good results. They did not have the part on hand. My second call resulted in the same outcome. My third call, to "7th Ave Appliance," yielded different results. They had the part I was looking for! I spoke with Tim Redlin, one of the owners of 7th Avenue Appliance, and after a number of cordial holiday exchanges, he informed me that the part would be $40.20 plus tax. I replied that I had seen that this part was typically running a little higher in price. I told him I would be by around 11:30 am to pick it up. He asked if I needed any help replacing the part, and I said I thought it looked pretty easy and would try tackling the job myself.

I was running a little late in picking the part up but managed to get to 7th Ave Appliance just after noon today. I walked in the door and Tim immediately greeted me with a big "Hello, are you Scott?" I let him know that I was there to pick up my part. He proceeded to tell me that he had the part I was looking for in a "universal" part number, which was quite a bit cheaper than the part he had initially told me about over the phone. I told him I would much rather pay just $15.91 for the same part! He had assumed so and already had the bill written up.

After I got home and replaced the part in the refrigerator (that is now working like a champ) my wife arrived home and I proceeded to tell her the story. She said that Tim could have easily charged us for the more expensive part. After all, Tim didn't get a service call out of the deal, just the price of the part. That's when I thought "How Fargo of You," Tim. In his honest way he was looking out for me, the customer, and not himself and the additional profit he could have made on the more expensive part.

I feel this story is quite indicative of the many people and businesses around the Fargo area. I know from experience as my wife and I grew up just south of Grand Forks, moved away for twelve years to Minneapolis, and made the move back to Fargo about the same time you moved to the area. There's nothing quite like the community of Fargo. It's a great place to be!

Scott Roller, Fargo

P.S. Shortly before going to press, I asked Scott for permission to use his story. He wrote back: "I'm happy to see you are including our story. You have my permission to use it. We recently moved to West Fargo and are in the throes of building a new house. Many similar Fargo stories have taken place during this process, all of which I'll be glad to share with you for your next book!

21.

Divine Light Special in Aisle Four

A wealth of kindness behind a cash register.

Last year, just before Christmas, I was shopping at the south side K-mart. After getting all the necessary things on my list, I proceeded to the check-out counter. A nice young man was there. When it came time to pay my bill, though, I realized I didn't have enough money with me. I was short about $2.50 so I said to the clerk: "I'm sorry, but I do not have enough money with me. Why don't you take back the hand lotion?"

He asked, "Are you sure?"

I replied, "Yes."

But instead of taking it back, he took out his own credit card from his pocket and scanned in the difference. When I got home I wrote to the manager of K-mart. I related how kind this young man was. I had his name from the invoice, so I was able to mention his name. I said that it isn't every day that you meet with such kindness and that he was really living the spirit of the Season. A few weeks later, I was back shopping at K-mart and I saw the young man at a check-out counter. I went over to him and I asked him if his manager had shown him the letter that I wrote.

He said, "No, but he put it on the bulletin board, and I am going to make a copy of it and take it home to frame it."

Sister Mary Fenton, Fargo

Editor's note: Of course, I had to ask Sister Mary the obvious question: "Were you wearing any religious garb when your story took place?"

"No, I wasn't wearing any religious garb or dress at the time. I usually wear lay clothing, so there is no way that anyone would know that I was a Religious Sister."

22.

Special Delivery

When your new son shares a birthday with your doctor's son,
something Fargo might happen.

At the end of my second pregnancy, I wasn't going into labor on
my own. I was feeling very large and round. I was ready to
have the baby. My first child had been delivered by C-section,
and I was really hoping to go into labor naturally and avoid the
scalpel for this one. I even found a great OB, Dr. Fiebiger, who
was supportive of my wishes; not all obstetricians are. Since I

was not progressing naturally, though, Dr. Fiebiger and I agreed on a date for labor to be induced.

The morning before coming in for the induction, I did as Dr. Fiebiger asked, and called the OB floor to make sure there was room for me. The nurse told me soberly, "I'm sorry, but there are already too many women in labor or who have just given birth; there are not enough beds for an elective induction." I would have to wait one more day.

The next morning, I called again. It was 7am. The nurse said in a hopeful voice, "We might have room if enough mothers discharge as expected today. Call back in two hours." I called back at 9 am, but there was still no room at the Inn. I was beginning to wonder if I was experiencing how Mary felt! Disappointed, I asked the nurse, "Should I call back tomorrow morning?" The nurse paused and explained carefully, "Your doctor is scheduled to go on vacation for a week. Tomorrow, the OB who will be on call is not comfortable inducing someone who has had a previous C-section. Dr. Fiebiger is willing to do the C-section for you later today, if you prefer." I asked if I could have some time to think it over, and she of course agreed.

I did not want to risk waiting a week for my physician to come back from vacation, possibly going into labor in her absence. My husband and I prayed and decided it would be best to have the C-section that day.

My husband and I arrived at the hospital later that afternoon. It had been a very busy day of deliveries and C-sections for Dr. Fiebiger. She pleasantly joked that she felt like she was a resident again, but made it clear she was still willing to do my C-section. It was a beautiful surgery; my husband was beside me. Dr. Fiebiger brought our precious, little son out of my womb. She lifted him over the sheet divider, and I saw his cute face and red hair. As they say around here, he was, "Oh, for cute!" and "Oh, for precious!" Then my husband took our son to another room with the nurses to get our little redhead cleaned up and measured.

While Dr. Fiebiger was sewing me back up, she was casually talking with the staff and me about various topics. I was grateful and relieved to have a way to keep my mind off of not being able to move most of my body from the epidural, not to mention my abdomen being stitched together. I felt surprisingly at ease.

A nurse asked the doctor, "Are you still going on vacation?" Dr. Fiebiger replied, "Yes, I am still going to go on vacation."

The nurse asked, "Where are you going?"

Dr. Fiebiger replied, "To see my son, Thomas. It's his twenty-first birthday, so I was going to fly to (some East coast city) to celebrate."

"Was going to?" the nurse asked.

"Well, my flight takes off at 6 pm."

I looked at the clock. It was 5:45!

She said something quickly, to the effect that it was not a big deal, and she would just catch the next flight.

I could not believe she had worked later just to help deliver my baby via C-section; she could have gone off to see her son, but she did not. Our baby could have been born the next day by C-section by another doctor. I was very, very grateful to have the OB whom I had seen for the previous nine months. I was touched.

When I heard Dr. Fiebiger talking about her son named "Thomas" in such a loving way, something clicked for me. My husband and I were debating whether or not to name our son Thomas or Lukas. My husband was favoring Thomas, and I had been favoring Lukas. When I saw that my son had bright red hair, I started to favor the name Thomas, too. Then, when I heard Dr. Fiebiger talk about her son in such a caring way, I liked how the name "Thomas" sounded.

After the surgery, when I was in the recovery room, I told my husband that Thomas was our son's name. He happily agreed! If I hadn't heard Dr. Fiebiger say, "Thomas," I don't know if I would have chosen that name.

Lots of other Fargo things have happened since we've been here, but this one, involving the birth of our son, is especially memorable.

Marie Hendrickson, Fargo

23.

The Flip Side

The Fargo Way creates a different kind of economy.
This can create big surprises for outsiders, both good and bad.

I was having lunch with Bruce Furness, a very popular former mayor of Fargo. He was about halfway through his meatloaf when he started telling me a story from his days in office.

"...so we were trying to get Cargill, the largest grain dealer in the world, to set up an office in Fargo," he was saying. "After a lot of hard work on the part of a lot of people, they finally agreed. They told us they'd need an office building capable of holding about two hundred people, to handle the workload, and asked if we could help find a good location. Pretty soon, the folks working for the city found them a very nice two-story building that was just what they wanted.

"The only problem was, about six months later I was talking to the Cargill folks again, and it turned out they hadn't filled the building. In fact, the second floor was still pretty empty.

"What's going on?" I asked. "Are there any problems?"

"'No,' they told me, 'but the hundred or so workers we've hired here in Fargo seem to be getting all the work done we usually need about two hundred for!' They just went on and on about the work ethic and competence level of the folks around here."

Bruce smiled at me, after another bite of meatloaf. "That stuff happens around here sometimes."

"It happens a lot," I said, working on my BLT. "There's just so many well-trained, high work-ethic people in Fargo, it's actually a much tougher job market than our low unemployment numbers reveal. Half the graduates who go away for big jobs in big cities come back once they start having kids, often taking huge cuts in pay to do it, just so their kids can grow up in a sane place."

"I know," Bruce said, "I read your chapter on the cab driver and his friends, who were all executives in other cities until they started having children and came back. I've seen examples of that myself. I think that's probably part of the reason Microsoft keeps growing so fast," he added, referring to the company's second-largest field campus on Earth, at the south end of Fargo. "It's not nearly as tough for them to find the people they need as it might be in other places with a three-point-five unemployment rate."

"Bruce?" I chimed in.

"Hmmm?" he tore his gaze from the last bite of meatloaf on his plate, waiting to be eaten.

"There are no other places with a three-point-five percent unemployment rate."

The Mayor smiled and took his last bite.

I had to add: "Not even our own state, North Dakota, with its oil boom in the west, has a three-point-five unemployment rate. Only Fargo has that."

"That's right," Bruce said. "Now, what would you like for dessert?"

Marc de Celle

24.

Interview with a Banker

Taking a sincere interest. No fangs.

I was in the businesslike, but distinctly non-opulent, office of Steve Swiontek, the head of Gate City Bank. Steve is a spry fiftysomething, very pleasant, quick to smile, quick to answer. Gate City is one of the largest banks in the state, with assets over $1 billion. It was May of 2012, and I'd asked to talk with him about local banking practices. After some brief chit-chat, I got to the reason I'd wanted to talk with him, even though I'd already spoken with a dozen other top bankers in North Dakota:

Marc: Thanks for seeing me, Steve. As I mentioned, I've spoken with the Mayor, and some economists at North Dakota State and the University of North Dakota, and with Cory Fong, the Tax Commissioner for North Dakota, and with Jim Gartin, head of the Fargo-Moorhead Economic Development Council, as well as Ralph Kingsbury, the long-time economics columnist for the Grand Forks Herald, and everyone agrees that the economic impact of the oil patch on the other side of the state hasn't affected Fargo's economy more than a couple of percentage points. There's widespread agreement amongst these experts that the single biggest factor behind Fargo's ability to sidestep the Great Recession was the absence of crazy Wall Street "mortgage products" coming into our area. This appears to be due solely to the ethics and caring of local bankers who refused to sell these products inappropriately, despite their potential profitability. Compared to where I'm from, I find this amazing. In Arizona, everyone I knew was getting at least a few phone calls a month from major banks pushing adjustable-rate loans. But the opposite seems to have happened here, where the local bankers acted as a bulwark against the onslaught of these toxic mortgages. And so, Fargo had no "Mortgage Meltdown" like the rest of the country, and without that meltdown, no Great Recession. The reason I want to talk to you is that I understand your bank not only didn't push these products, but you never even sold any of the mortgages you wrote back to Wall Street. Is that true?

Steve: Yes, it is, Marc. We didn't. We like keeping things in-house. If we provide a mortgage, we believe in it.

Marc: Well, according to my research, a lot of banks around here must not have sold mortgages they didn't believe in, either. According to the Pew Research Center, North Dakota has far and away the lowest projected foreclosure rate from the subprime mortgage mess of any state in the country. They have projected just one out of every hundred and sixty-five mortgages in North Dakota will be foreclosed. The second best state is South Dakota, with only one out of every hundred and sixteen projected to fail, and third is West Virginia, with one out of every eighty-nine mortgages expected to be foreclosed. So North Dakota has nearly half the rate of foreclosure of the third best state in the country. That's a huge separation from every state except South Dakota, and North Dakota's almost thirty percent better than they are. Why do you think that is?

Steve: Well, I think there's a tradition of people looking after one another around here. So at our bank, we always just try to find the best possible mortgage for the person. Also, I think people who grew up on farms around here are very conservative. They want something that will last through the bad times, the snows, the droughts, the lean years. And we all think that way, and we all try to look after each other.

169

Marc: Back in Arizona, starting sometime in two-thousand-two, my wife and I, and all our friends as well, started getting phone calls from big-name banks trying to sell us adjustable-rate mortgages. By two-thousand-four, we were getting one or two of these phone calls every week! From the biggest banks in the country! We already had a decent fixed-rate mortgage and we were happy in our home, but we were constantly bombarded by these huge banks trying to get us into some kind of new-fangled mortgage and take equity out of our home or buy a home twice as big. It was craziness. I mean, fixed rates were about the lowest they'd been in thirty years, and I remember hearing a report on NPR at that time that most of the mortgages being sold in the country were adjustable-rate mortgages, with monthly payments that were going to get much larger in two or three years! It seemed inevitable that we were going to end up with a glut of foreclosures when those balloon payments hit a couple of years down the line, but in the meantime real estate prices were skyrocketing with all the new homebuilding being driven by all these huge mortgages being sold to people who weren't going to be able to afford them in the long run. Didn't any of that happen here?

Steve: Well, there were a few outsiders who came in and tried to start selling some of those kinds of mortgages, but we did our best to try to stop it, so they didn't stick around.

Marc: What do you mean? Did you and other local bankers threaten to break their legs or something? Take them out hunting and have an accident?

Steve: (laughing). No, but we did tell them we didn't like what they were doing, and we were starting to talk with people about it, from reporters to people in government, and pretty soon they just left.

Marc: Sounds like you did it the Fargo Way, *'You know, I went to grade school with the economics reporter at the paper, and I just might pay him a visit and tell him I think he ought to look into what you're doing...'*

Steve: (laughing). Yeah. We did some things like that. But I think they were having trouble anyway. People are pretty conservative around here. They develop long-term relationships with their bankers, so new folks coming in selling strange new kinds of mortgages probably weren't going to get very far anyway.

Marc: What about the big-name banks? Back in Arizona and California, they were the ones making the big push for this stuff. Why didn't they do the same pushy stuff up here?

Steve: Well, first of all, there's only one big national bank that already has branches here, and almost all their executives are local people who grew up around here, so I'd guess that was part of it. And maybe the other big banks were just too busy in other parts of the country to try coming up here, with our small population. But really, I don't think they would have done well if they had. People like to stick with what they know around here. Maybe they had good research that told them not to bother!

We both laughed. That was the end of the interview. He'd told me what I needed to know.

A few weeks later, I saw Steve in his car, driving around downtown Fargo. I didn't catch the exact make, but it was a very non-descript mid-sized car, not remotely a luxury model.

Did I mention he's the Chairman, President and CEO of the fourth largest bank in North Dakota?

That kind of non-show-offy frugality is not the exception around here. It's the rule. And it lies near the heart of the Fargo Way.

And it's more important than you think. The lack of ostentation – or rather, the frequent shunning of ostentation – may lie at the core of the Fargo Way.

I've saved that story for last.

25.

The Seamstress Sews It up

Frugality empowers the creation of real value.

I'd known the Seamstress for a less than a year.

I was on the couch in her living room. She was sitting on the chair across from me, sewing something. My daughter, Anastasia, was in a back bedroom trying something on.

My book, *How Fargo of You*, had just come out. The Seamstress had read it, and we were having a nice chat about things Fargo.

I don't remember what led up to it, but she proceeded to clue me in on a huge piece of the Fargo puzzle I hadn't yet seen. Like all things Fargo, it had been hidden right out in the open all along. It was just so foreign to my thinking I couldn't grasp what I was looking at.

"Oh, I was just talking with this lady the other day who sells boats out in the lakes country" – the 'lakes country' takes up about a third of Minnesota and lies just thirty miles east of Fargo – it's the core of that state's 'Land of 10,000 Lakes' motto, which is, believe it or not, no exaggeration – "and she was telling me that when people buy a new boat, they'll often ask her to leave it out for a week before they come back, so it won't look quite so expensive when they bring their friends or family with them to pick it up."

"What?" I said, incredulously. It was so opposite from what I'd grown up with in California and Arizona, people constantly trying to outdo each other with their latest purchases.

The Seamstress let out a little giggle. "Oh, I know, but people around here don't want to call too much attention to themselves…"

"Well, I'd noticed that there are far fewer luxury cars on the road here than in California and Arizona," I said, "even though I know from the economic studies I've seen that North Dakota may have more millionaires per capita than any other state, and there are a lot more people per capita who could afford them."

"Right," the Seamstress said. "And people don't go crazy with their houses, either. My next-door neighbor is a Professor

Emeritus from NDSU who's lived there for decades. He could obviously afford a lot more house. Raised his family here. They like the neighborhood. Why move?"

Hmmm. The Seamstress lived in a very nice, forty-year-old neighborhood, average house size under 2,000 square feet.

My whole concept of how the economic world works and what drives people to acquire stuff was shifting inside my head. I finally managed to blurt out: "Are you kidding me?"

"No, and there's a surgeon just two blocks over who lived there for more than twenty years. People like the neighborhood, so why move? He even turned down a lot of opportunities to move to more prestigious jobs. I don't think he was willing to give up the great schools and environment his kids had. 'For Sale' signs rarely go up around here."

"Man, that is so different from Hollywood and Scottsdale and the other places I've lived," I said, shaking my head. "There, the whole point was to get a bigger house and a fancier car and a shinier boat and show it off to prove... well, I guess they were trying to prove they were better than everyone else..."

"No one wants to prove that here," the Wise Seamstress said, flatly. Then she giggled. "Because no one – well, almost no one – believes it."

My head grasping for something to hold onto, I thought of a reference point from the past, pre-Fargo. "I remember doing some market research in the 1980s for a large bank in Arizona," I said, "and it turned out that the average asset level per household in Scottsdale, which was already becoming known as

"Snotsdale" and "the Beverly Hills of the Desert," was lower than the average asset level in some other parts of the Phoenix area where the houses were much plainer and smaller and there were far fewer luxury cars and so on. And I remember being surprised. But now I guess that might explain a lot."

"It's all about what people value," the Wise Seamstress said. "And I think most of us start to pick that up pretty early in our childhood from what we see around us..."

My head was still swimming. The Seamstress was casually undoing what she was describing to me... flipping assumptions picked up in my youth like so many pancakes...

Anastasia emerged from the back of the house and did a few pirouettes. Verdict: Her new figure skating outfit looked great. She left to get back into her street clothes.

Suddenly, it hit me between the eyes. "So back in Scottsdale, they have big fancy houses and cars, and are often just scraping by. They've got to work a lot of hours just to keep payments made, probably can't spend a lot of time with their kids, but instead they're sending them to fancy classes – *Oh!* And when a funky business deal comes across their desk that might make them a lot of money – like all the crazy mortgages Wall Street started putting out a decade ago, for instance, *they don't think twice! They can't afford to! They're freakin' desperate.* They sell that stuff like there's no tomorrow, and justify it every which way from Sunday."

The Seamstress was nodding.

"But your neighbors are in exactly the opposite position. They're free to do what they think is right, because they haven't invested in stuff, they've invested in their own freedom and security and relationships and happiness. Instead of big houses and fancy cars, they've undoubtedly got small houses, nondescript cars, and what you don't see are the big bank accounts and fancy portfolios. They've invested in their own ability to make choices!

Still nodding.

"Like everything else in Fargo, it's *Opposite World!*" I was getting loud and excited. The Wise Seamstress giggled.

I spread my arms apart, my jaw slack. "And that's the real reason the bankers here never tried to sell the crazy mortgages coming out of Wall Street. *They didn't have to, and their value system is such that they didn't want to!* Their lifestyles are built around buying themselves the freedom and security to do what they think is right!" Little did I know how right I was – it would be another year before I recognized Steve Swiontek, Chairman, President and CEO of the $1 billion-in-assets Gate City Bank, driving his totally non-descript little mid-sized car around town.

"I think so," the Wise Seamstress nodded, as my daughter emerged, ready to go.

"Oh, man!" I said. "It's the frugality around here that powers all the kindness and generosity I've been writing about!"

"Oh, sure," said the Seamstress, as if I'd just stated the most obvious thing in all the world. "What else could it be?"

I don't think I could have learned much, if any of that, from a sociologist. I know a few. Some are friends of mine. At least one is brilliant (grew up in North Dakota, too.) But I just don't think their subject is far enough along yet to grasp Fargo. If it were, they'd be helping us make a lot more Fargos in other places. We could use them.

But I think there's a Seamstress who really understands what makes this place tick. And, I suspect, a lot of others around here who get it, too. To them, it's obvious.

I'm telling you, it's a different planet around here.

Marc de Celle

Book III

Zero Degrees of Separation

Mapping the Space-Time-Family-Friends-Community Continuum.

1.

Ownership Connections

*A lot of home-growns are continuously updating
a five-dimensional map in their heads.*

I remember the moment it finally started to dawn on me.

"Here, let me show you something." Keith took a few steps to his right, gesturing toward an old photo of a baseball team sitting on his bookcase. The men comprising the team were healthy and robust, and looked to be between the ages of twenty and forty. Pointing to one of the figures, he said, "That's my grandfather, Peter, and his teammates are all his brothers."

"Wow!" I said.

"The photo was taken in 1912 in Ray, North Dakota, and that," he said, pointing to another man on the team, "was Bob's grandad."

"Oh," I said. Keith was referring to North Dakota State Senate Majority Leader Bob Stenehjem, who had just recently died in a car accident while on a hunting trip in Alaska. I had prompted this conversation a minute earlier by asking Keith if they'd been related.

Keith's last name was also Stenehjem, which had prompted my question. We'd just been introduced a couple of minutes earlier, in his office. Keith is the Vice President of Academic Affairs at Mayville State University, which is the perfect place to begin talking about Zero Degrees of Separation.

But right that moment, I couldn't take my eyes off the old photo. I started peppering Keith with questions. Keith could not only tell me the names of his great uncles, he could tell me where most had ended up, in either North Dakota or Minnesota, as young men, what paths their careers had taken, who they had married and the names of their children and what many of the progeny of his generation were doing now...

He had this huge map in his head! It seemed to be this 3D image centered around our region, and each of the men in this photograph had started from a mutual point on it, traveled through it, ending up somewhere in it...

But wait, that meant the map also moved through time, showing where all these people, their spouses and progeny had all been at any given moment... then their progeny... it was a 4D map!

...But wait! It included the personalities of these people, who their friends had been or were, what their communities had been and were still like...

It was 5D!

And suddenly I realized I'd heard this, or hints of it, a hundred times since moving to North Dakota, but hadn't ever made sense of it. But there was something about having that photograph of that sibling-only baseball team, all those once-young men looking at me through time, and one of their many offsprings' offspring standing in front of me telling me about how they and their families had moved through and changed the world around them since – and it all clicked:

This guy owns this place. The whole region. He's got it mapped out, where everyone in or near his family was and is and who they were and are and when they were there and where they are now and what their friends and communities were and are, across the whole of the Northern Prairie over the last century or so. This region isn't someplace he happens to be. It's his place and their place and their friends' and communities' place and he knows it all like the back of his hand. He's got it all mapped out in a friendly space-time-family-friends and community continuum...

And I realized this was true of a great number – perhaps a majority – of all the multi-generational locals I'd ever met. An early booksigning I'd done flashed into my mind. It had been, ironically, at the Historical and Cultural Center of Clay County, on the Minnesota side of the Red River across from Fargo. There had been about twenty people waiting to get their books signed. The line ran alongside a full-sized Viking ship, the Hjemkomst, which had been sailed from Duluth, Minnesota to Norway in the early 1980s. As I was signing, I'd heard a lot of chatter in the line amongst people who were obviously strangers – but not for long:

"So, where are you from?"

"My family's from just south of Carrington. I live in Fargo now. How about you?"

"I grew up in Casselton, but I currently live in Moorhead. Say – Carrington – do you know the Eastman's?"

"I went to school with Karen Eastman..."

"I know Karen! She's my cousin's best friend!..."

These people had been happily adding onto their maps while they waited in line for me to sign their books! Now, in Keith's office, standing before the humble baseball shrine to his ancestors, I realized: *They all own this place! Lock, stock and barrel! No wonder they behave the way they do!*

No one living in L.A., where I spent more than a decade of my life, feels like they own that place. Not that I ever met. Not even the mayor. It's a sea of chaos within which you try to carve out a niche and hunker down with a relatively small group of family, friends and associates and do your best to feel safe. The same has become increasingly true of Phoenix over the years, which, by the late '80s had begun to remind me of L.A.

But of course, those two places never had much of an established community or culture in the first place. Their entire histories could be best described with one word: *influx.*

Driving back to Fargo from Mayville later that day, I started chuckling. I was remembering a little impromptu research project I'd done a couple of years earlier. I'd started randomly comparing experiences with other newcomers to the Fargo area, whenever I came across them.

When I met someone who'd moved here fairly recently as an adult, I'd ask something like, "So, what's your experience of Fargo been like?"

Everyone I'd asked had told me stories similar to my own. With one exception. It was a young couple who'd moved here from an area known for heavy accents, and the lady had told me: "Well, my husband and I are from (omitted), and especially him, his accent is heavier than mine, he gets asked all the time, 'Where are you from?' you know, like saying 'You're not from around here, are you?' I mean, it's just *so* rude."

At the time, I can remember thinking, *Well, I've been asked that a lot, too. Just never thought anything of it. Maybe if I had a heavy accent, I'd take it differently.*

Now, laughing to myself on the way back from Mayville, I wanted to reach back in time and say to her, "Everyone asks that same question of everyone around here, lady! It has nothing to do with accents! They're just busy trying to add on to their Space-Time-Family-Friends-Community Continuum maps!"

Like Keith's map, all these maps start close to home, and then spread out, reaching surprising distances over time.

So let's do that. Let's start close to home and move outwards.

2.

Cat on a Hot Tin Screen

Okay, maybe not tin. Or even hot.
There was, however, a screen with a cat on it.

I glanced out my bedroom window. I was in college and living at home in Fargo with my parents, and my window faced the next door neighbor's front door – my parent's house is a rambler and the neighbor's is "L" shaped. Anyway, something caught my eye. There was something strange on the window next to the front door of the neighbor's house, some kind of big blob... Wait! It was the neighbor's cat hanging on the screen inside the house! It was summertime and I assumed the cat was jumping after flies, on the screen, as flies are numerous in the summer and always trying to get into houses – and as you noted in How Fargo of You, North Dakota flies are formidable, and often get what they want!

So, I thought nothing of this, thinking the cat would get off the screen and go about her business. I left the bedroom and went about my own business. About 20 minutes later, though, I got this feeling that I should recheck on the cat. Looking out my bedroom window again, I saw the cat still hanging on the screen! In the same position! "The poor thing must be stuck!" I realized!

I quickly walked out of the house and went over to the neighbor's house. I talked to the cat through the screen, who looked pretty shaken up and exhausted from the whole ordeal. I knocked on the door. No answer. I rang the bell, it didn't work which is quite common around these parts – below zero kills cheap doorbells, I think. I knocked again. Still no answer. The main door was ajar, and upon checking the screen door, I found it unlocked. I yelled inside, "Sue, Greg, are you here?" No answer. Again I yelled, "Hello, is anyone here?" Still no answer.

I felt a little uncomfortable just walking into someone else's house, but I had to help the cat. I was hoping I didn't meet up with the neighbors walking around in their underwear, or worse! So, I cautiously headed back to the bedroom I knew the cat was in – I'd been in Sue and Greg's house before – and found her very happy to see me. I carefully pried her nails out of the screen, and once she was free, gave her a quick hug. She took off to another part of the house.

Thus, doing my good deed for the day, I walked out of the house and headed for home. I told my mother all about it when I got back. The next day, I walked over to the neighbor's with my nail trimmer (I was going to college for Veterinary Technology at NDSU at the time). I knocked on the door and this time, Sue answered right away. "Hi, Sue. Did you know I was in your house yesterday?" I asked.

She said, "No, I didn't. What was up?" I told her what had happened, and explained I would like to trim the cat's nails so the cat wouldn't get stuck again, anytime soon.

Sue guessed that she and Greg had been downstairs when I'd come over, watching television, and didn't hear me knock.

So I trimmed her cat's nails, which the cat didn't like very much, and was offered a pop for my troubles. We had a nice visit, and I returned home.

I still think of this story once in a while. If this happened anywhere else, someone walking into someone else's house might get shot or arrested!

Toni Grabinger, Lake Park, Minnesota

Editor's Note: Hmmm. Maybe it's a space-time-family-friends-community-and-animals continuum. Actually, for a lot of people around here, it probably is.

3.

Snow Shoveling Mob

Ignited by spontaneous compassion.

As a teenager in Minot, North Dakota, I experienced a few huge snowfalls. I want to tell you about one, not the largest, but for me, the most memorable.

About 24 inches of snow had fallen during the night, and I was told by my parents I couldn't do anything that day until the sidewalk and driveway were shoveled. Before I got outside, though, my mom was reading in the paper about people having heart attacks from shoveling snow, and told me to take it easy.

I was 15 years old and had the snow cleared quickly. I came in to warm up, then called my friend. But he couldn't do anything until his driveway was shoveled either, he told me, and he hadn't started yet. He lived less than a block away, so I said I would help him. As I got to the next street on my way, though, I saw an old man shoveling his drive. He was panting and his face was the reddest I had ever seen. He might not have been in his eighties, but I was a teenager and anyone older than forty was an old man. He wasn't clutching his chest yet – but he looked pretty close! Remembering my mother's caution about heart attacks, I knew I had to help, so I asked him to take a break and as I had my shovel, I started digging.

The man across the street saw this and came over, too. When the man in the driveway next to him saw his neighbor heading over, he joined us as well. The three of us cleared that driveway quickly, and the old man thanked us and went inside. Then we all went across the street to do the first guy's driveway. About that time, the old man's neighbor had come out to start his driveway, but saw us all crossing the street together, snow shovels in hand, and joined us.

By the time I got to my friend's house, seven of us were clearing driveways, one after another! When we finished my friend's driveway, we noticed the next few driveways were already cleared.

We were shaking hands and disbanding when a lady, whose drive had already been cleared before we got there, came out and said, "Wait, don't go yet. Come up here." We went to her already cleared driveway a little bewildered, when she came back out with a tray of sandwiches and cocoa. She said, "I saw what you were doing and thought you could use this."

Doug Beierle, West Fargo

4.

The Home Town I've Never Lived in

...a shot of ?????

These offerings are from a small, very small town, about an hour north of Bismarck, by the name of Mercer. My late father was raised on a family farm in this area. He left the farm, as that was not his desired line of work. He joined the Army, fought in Korea, and made a living for his family as a bookkeeper, for some years in Wisconsin, but the majority in Minnesota. We always made at least one trip a year to North Dakota, for two weeks of visiting relatives, sightseeing, and going to Brush Lake.

After my father retired he moved back to this small town and bought the house that his mother had lived in, which was built by his father. He lived there so he could help his mother and reconnect with his siblings. Sad to say, the time came when grandma passed away, and my siblings and I, who were living in Minnesota, came back for the funeral.

Grandma had many children who in turn had many children of their own. There was the potential for a shortage of lodging in Mercer for those who came back for the funeral. Out of the blue, one of the townspeople offered up beds to my family, which was at the time me, my husband and two little kids. This was offered without any thought on her part. We didn't take her up on her offer, as we'd planned to stay with my father, as did my siblings and their children. We never needed that nice lady's beds, but I still remember her generous offer very clearly.

Now jump ahead several years to my father's funeral. He had moved back to Minnesota when he became ill, so my siblings and I could help care for him. The circle of life, I guess. But he was buried in the Mercer cemetery with the rest of his family, and his funeral was at his home church, in Mercer. This time, we were a house short, because when my dad moved back to Minnesota he had sold the house in North Dakota. Regardless, we all went back for the funeral, in the midst of a March, 2009 blizzard. This time, another set of neighbors, who owned a property that they rented out to lake goers and hunters, made the offer of housing to my two sisters and one brother-in-law, free of charge.

My kids and I go back to Mercer a minimum of once a year, and on occasion, I have gone back as many as three times a year. Visiting "my people" in Mercer and the area is like a shot of ??????. You fill in the blank, I don't know the right word. I feel totally at home, totally loved, totally comfortable, and totally rejuvenated after my time there.

I love North Dakota.

LeAnn Schreiber, Winona, Minnesota

5.

Disaster Strikes, Help Follows

Like clockwork.

Our family was on vacation in Colorado in the summer of 2000, and there was a freak rainstorm that hit Fargo one night – 8 inches in 7 hours! Our neighbors could see that our home was the only one without lights on that night, but there was nothing they could do, as they were fighting their own fight in their own basements. Sump pumps failed, electricity was spotty and sewage was backing up into homes. We arrived home from vacation to find our basement had been submerged in a full 17 inches of sewage, although it had been pumped out, due to the kindness of Fargo friends who had come over and started the sump pump up again before we got home, once the storm was over and the electricity was fully back on.

We had to get everything out of the basement and cut the sheetrock out at least four feet up on all the walls. But word spread quickly about our circumstances, and within two days we had the basement cleared by friends and family; sheetrock cut away four feet up the wall; the basement power washed and disinfected; our carpet guy Bruce had heard about it and came by to re-measure and offered us a great deal on new carpeting; and our builders had heard and came by to offer assistance... so much assistance that our home was put back together (minus the belongings that had to be thrown due to being exposed to sewage) all within two weeks of the storm! And of course, through the first couple of days after our return, we had people bringing over food and offering to watch our daughter Emma, who was just one at the time, while we worked to get things sorted and thrown away. Amazing! We felt so blessed at the time and knew then, although we had known already, we knew then even more what a special place Fargo was.

I realize that you are probably in the middle of a blizzard right now...yes, I still read the local Fargo news on a daily basis after ten years of being away...

We moved from Fargo to Phoenix.... just the opposite of what you did! When Lutheran Health Systems merged with Samaritan Health System of Phoenix, my husband Dennis had to move to Phoenix in order to keep his position. The merger made a lot of sense from a business perspective, but on a personal level we were sad to move, as Dennis grew up in North Dakota and his family is mostly in the Grand Forks area, and I grew up in Wisconsin and my family is there and in Minneapolis.

I have been thinking about writing a book "How Phoenix of You," but I think a better title might be a phrase that we hear from so many of our friends here: "You're not in Fargo Anymore..." But of course, like all Fargoans, we still have lots of lifelong friends from the Northern Prairie that either visit us, or we visit them, on an annual basis.

Mary Dahlen, Phoenix, Arizona

6.

A Fargo Welcome

Howdy, neighbor.

About 31 years ago, we moved back to Fargo. We were unloading the truck when our new next door neighbor, Carol, brought lunch to us, along with dessert. I remember when she came over, my three sons were all up in the tree in our new front yard, which was typical of the monkeys that they were when they were 5, 7, and 10. Carol saved the day for us with that lunch! Carol and her husband, Bill, shared their summer garden produce with us that year as well. They came to be some of my best friends, a friendship that has lasted through the years. We still stay in touch, not as often we should; but I know I can call on them at any time.

We had moved many times in the years before we came back to Fargo, but that was the first and only time we received a wonderfully warm welcome anything like that! Carol and Bill are the kind of people that do lasting and kind deeds so often that I'm sure there are many people who could say, "How Fargo of you!" about them!

Donna Chmelar, Echo, Minnesota

7.

Prom Angel

He met her on the way there.

It was a beautiful spring Saturday in 1998, and my son Chad was a high school senior. He had spent all day washing and cleaning his car, getting it ready to go to a Prom in Aberdeen, South Dakota, about eighty miles away, at the high school his girlfriend attended.

He left home just in time to get to Aberdeen to go out to dinner with her, and then on to the Prom at Aberdeen High School. But he only made it as far as the convenience store in

Edgeley, North Dakota, about 60 miles north of Aberdeen. He was having car trouble – it had basically died – and called me from there.

I drove there with our old car – a car I was afraid would not make it to Aberdeen. Chad's Dad was in Jamestown, North Dakota, forty miles in another direction, at work with our good family car. The convenience store in Edgeley had a small coffee shop, so when I arrived, we sat down to talk over the situation.

So there we were, sitting in the convenience store, my son dressed in a black tuxedo, and we have no car to get him to Aberdeen. We also have no time to spare; if he doesn't leave soon, he'll be late. We were trying to come up with a solution that would get him to Aberdeen in time, but we were getting nowhere.

A young woman from Edgeley simply walks over to our table and hands my son her car keys. Now this woman and I are acquaintances – we had gone to the same high school, but many years apart. We had last run into each other maybe a couple of years earlier, very briefly. But she did not know my son at all.

She had been sitting at a nearby table having coffee with a group of women, but of course, could hear what was going on. (Small town coffee shop!)

She was truly our Angel that day! She told Chad to use her car and just leave it at the convenience store with the keys under the mat when he got back from the Prom.

So, Sunday morning, as he was filling her car with gas at that convenience store and getting ready to call us to come pick him up, a pastor also stopped to fill his car before driving to the church he was going to speak at that morning. The church was in Jud, where we live – so he gave Chad a ride home!

Sharman Zachrison, Jud, North Dakota

8.

Riding in the Rumble Seat

A trip down memory lane from a stranger.

Every year, my dad loved to attend the Old Thresher's Reunion in Rollag, Minnesota, just about twenty miles east of Fargo. He enjoyed visiting with the other farmers and seeing the old steam threshers they used harvest with, in the days before gasoline engines, and all the other great old cars and machines. But one year, the Old Thresher's Reunion had a real surprise for him.

It was the reunion in October of 1982. Dad started visiting with a man who had come with a beautifully restored Model A

Ford. Dad told him that was the same kind of car he drove when he was first married fifty years ago. In fact, my dad told him, he and mom would be celebrating their Fiftieth Anniversary the very next next week.

The man told dad to take the car for the whole weekend! Dad said no, he couldn't do that, insisting "You don't even know me!" But the man insisted harder. As I recall it, dad wanted to leave his car with the man, but he also said no to that, saying it wasn't necessary.

So we all got to enjoy that old Model A Ford. What a fun time we had, each of us kids and grandkids getting a ride in the rumble seat. We have a lot of pictures from that anniversary weekend, all taking turns riding around in that beautiful old car. In fact, as a gift to mom and dad when they moved off the farm a few years later, the whole family had my husband paint a watercolor picture of their old place, and he added the car into the scene.

Donna McKelvey,St. Johns, Michigan

9.

It's a Small Nodak World

Even beyond North Dakota.

I finished your book **How Fargo of You** on the flight back to Greeley, Colorado, from my Fortieth Bismarck High School reunion. Interesting. Something all of of us North Dakotans (NoDaks) have always known, but have never seen in print. Thank you.

One topic you might ponder should you do a next edition, is how we former NoDaks seem to connect and find each other in our "foreign lands" such as Colorado.

For example, my trusted plumber is a guy from Langdon, North Dakota. My colleagues at Aims Community College here in Colorado include my French teacher from Valley City, North Dakota; the head of the Counseling Department is from Bismarck; the recently retired music professor is from Bismarck; the former chair of the auto repair program is from Grand Forks; the head of the economics department is a farm boy whose Colorado license plates read NDSU; one of my former doctoral dissertation committee members; and former board member at Aims is a UND graduate. I could go on and on and on....

Last year at a University of Northern Colorado – University of North Dakota football game I wore a UND hockey cap and a UNC sweatshirt. All of the UND green folks were looking at me and yelling, "Make up your mind!"

While many of us leave North Dakota, I guess we always keep it close to us. And with the small population there, even if we're a thousand miles from the state, if we meet another NoDaker, we always tend to talk a few minutes until we realize we know some of the same folks.

My dad was a North Dakota native farmboy who came back to his home state to take over pathology at various North Dakota hospitals. One night, when I went to dinner with him in Bismarck, a guy stopped by our table to chat casually. I asked, later, "Who was that fellow?"

"Oh, that was the state governor, Governor Jim Guy." Some other fellow stopped by after that, who happened to be one of the state senators.... where else do you causally bump into such people other than North Dakota?

Good luck with your next book, Marc. Nice to see some of these strange NoDak phenomena finally making it into print!

Ralph Tarnasky
Chair, World Languages and Ethnic Studies
Aims Community College, Colorado

10.

North Dakota Drivers

Taking the state of euphoria beyond its customary borders.

I prefer driving instead of flying, because I like to see things, and flying makes me really sick. While driving, I always like to look at license plates, always looking for the familiar one from North Dakota. One time, while driving through Wyoming on my way to Las Vegas, I passed a semi truck with North Dakota license plates. As I did, he honked his horn and started waving and I waved back, both of us with huge smiles on our faces. We were both so happy to see someone else from North Dakota!

Whenever I tell anyone from another state about this, they don't seem to understand. They always ask if I knew him, and of course the answer is no. I have no idea who he was and I don't know if I have ever seen him since. But the warm feeling I had when he shared a greeting with me and I returned the greeting to another NoDak-er, many states away, in the middle of a big old interstate highway, is just amazing. It was just like seeing an old friend even though it was someone I had never met.

You might think this is an isolated incident, but a couple of years ago, while going through Oklahoma on my way to Texas, I passed a car with North Dakota license plates. They sped up to get alongside me and we waved and smiled at each other in a very excited, exuberant manner... I'm sure some other drivers thought we were crazy people ~ but once again, it was like seeing family or an old friend, even though I have no idea who those people were or which part of the state they were from. I'd been out of the state less then 24 hours and the joy I felt seeing a car with people from North Dakota was overwhelming.

I was traveling to Texas because my sister has lived in Austin for almost 30 years – and she says she still gets the same feeling! When she sees the familiar plate from North Dakota, she wants to run up to them and say hi; but refrains because she has nothing on her that identifies her as being from there; like she says, the poor people would think they were getting robbed or something. Most people we share this with think it is such an odd thing, except when I tell someone from North Dakota, they always seem to get it.

Weird, huh? Unless you're from North Dakota!

Janell Schmidt, Fargo

11.

That's a Long Way to Go for a Dakota Repair Job

Finding Fargo in Oregon.

It started the day after an enjoyable Thanksgiving here in Grafton, North Dakota, with our younger son Mark and his wife Rhonda. We began packing our SUV for our annual visit to Oregon, where our granddaughters play basketball during the winter, and we love watching and experiencing their excitement.

By noon, the vehicle was nearly full, with my wife, Marilyn, putting the last parcels in. The garage door was closed, and just inside the garage, the rear door of the SUV was open – which, as many people with vans or SUVs know, is a disaster waiting to happen.

It happened.

I had just parked our other car outside, and without thinking, I pushed the garage door opener and started toward the house.

Marilyn's scream alerted me that something was wrong. As I looked up, I saw the garage door still rising, entangled with the rear door of the SUV. The bottom panel of the SUV door slowly ripped off. By the time the garage door was fully open, the bottom panel of the rear SUV door was hanging from it! We were scheduled to leave for Oregon early the next morning. The SUV door would still shut and latch, but it looked like the rear of a "Demolition Derby" car.

It was just past noon when I called the local dealership's body shop in Grand Forks. I told them what had happened and asked if I could bring the vehicle in to have them look at it and, if possible, reattach the panel to the door. They told me to bring it in, and a minute later I put the torn panel in the SUV and was on my way to Grand Forks.

The estimate was just under $1,000 and yes, they could fix it, but not for three days. Latches, clips, screws, etc. would have to be ordered, and shop was already busy. We were leaving for Oregon early tomorrow. Three days would not work!

Marilyn and I made the decision to take the door panel with us and get it fixed when we got to Oregon. The next morning, with the panel touching the SUV roof and making it impossible to see out of the rear view mirror, we started our westward trip. I could only use the side mirrors and was not completely certain the rear door would stay shut. The rear of our SUV looked as though it had been in an accident. It had!

We arrived in Hillsboro, a Portland suburb of about 100,000, just past noon, on December 1, 2009. We had an apartment to move into, a basketball game to see that night, Christmas shopping to do and family functions to attend. When and where would we get our SUV fixed?

Oh, well. We'd have to deal with that later. It was time to see our son, Dr. Lance Anderson, his wonderful wife Kelly, also from North Dakota, and our granddaughters Sloan, Marly and Abby.

We soon learned that Lance knew of a body shop owner. This man, he said, had sponsored the amateur basketball team he had played on while attending Pacific University. The man's name was Bruce, and he had moved to Oregon in the 1960s, Lance told me, from North Dakota.

I was pretty sure I had found the place to have my vehicle fixed.

I called Bruce's Body Shop and asked if he would take a look at a damaged rear door on a Honda SUV. I was told to bring it in the next morning and he would see what he could do. I went to the shop the next morning. The interior was full of cars

216

being worked on by three busy men. After a short wait, one of the men approached me, extended his hand and said "Hi, I'm Bruce. How can I help you?"

We went outside, where I showed him my damaged SUV. Before I could tell him my story or where I was from, he noticed the North Dakota plates. The stories and small talk began immediately. As is usually the case when two North Dakotans meet in a distant place, they find they have much in common, have been to the same places, and know or at least know of, some of the same people.

His name was Bruce Graumann. He was originally from Harvey, North Dakota, and he had grown up on a farm in Pony Gulch Township. I had measured wheat acreage there for the County Agricultural office. I had taught and coached in nearby Fessenden. His nephew had played on Harvey teams I had coached against. Another of his relatives was a well-known school superindent whom I knew.

Eventually we got back to the SUV door. "Can you fix it?" I asked. He told me if I left it at the shop overnight and came back at noon the next day, he would have it ready to go. I was surprised. I asked about acquiring parts and labor time. He replied, simply, "Not to worry," it will be done. I thanked him and told him Lance would bring me back during his noon break the next day.

Lance and I returned at noon the next day. As we entered the shop, Bruce announced to his men that "The best three-point shooter in Oregon and his dad from North Dakota are here!"

After some good natured banter, Lance left for work and Bruce brought me out to examine the SUV.

My vehicle looked good as new. Bruce proudly opened and shut the rear door and had me examine it to check the solidness of the back panel. He had done marvelous work! We went back into the shop and his small office. I took out my checkbook and asked him what I owed him.

He put his hand on my shoulder and said I owed him nothing. I looked at him in surprise and disbelief and said "That can't be right. You needed new parts and worked after hours to get it done."

He replied that he had "used clamps, latches, and screws on hand" and that he often stayed after hours. He smiled and said, "You were in a bind, I like you, and we're both from North Dakota. No charge."

He then suggested that I could pay him by attending his church's Christmas program the next evening. I said "I wish I could, but I have a commitment to watch my granddaughter play basketball the next two evenings in a tournament." As I left, I thanked him again and said I would find a way to repay his kindness.

That evening, as Marilyn and I talked in our apartment, Marilyn decided to repay Bruce by baking a large batch of Christmas cookies and bringing them to Bruce at the shop.

The next morning, Marilyn and our youngest grand-daughter, Abby, 9 years old, baked the cookies. That afternoon, we visited Bruce and his men at the shop. Marilyn presented the cookies, thanked Bruce and wished him and his shop men a Merry Christmas. Bruce seemed overjoyed that Marilyn had done this small act of kindness. Compared to what he had done for us it was a small, but he was genuinely touched. We shared cookies and conversation for about an hour. Upon leaving, we mentioned we would be attending our granddaughter Marly's ball games the next two nights.

Two nights later, after arriving at the gym, we started up the bleacher steps toward the cheering section when we heard a familiar voice boom out, "Hi, I'm glad to see you could make it." Bruce had remembered our granddaughter was playing ball and had traveled across town to watch her.

It still amazes me that a man I did not know could show such kindness and friendship.

People have left North Dakota over the decades, seeking new opportunities. Their moving has been North Dakota's loss and their new home state's gain. They brought with them their "How Fargo of You" behavior and still display it in distant places.

Gene and Marilyn Anderson, Grafton, North Dakota

219

12.

Distant Relations

North Dakotans in Singapore.

My sons were attending the Singapore American School when a new superintendent was hired. One Bob Gross, from Napoleon, North Dakota, not 15 miles away from where I was born. Bob had retained a heavy German brogue from an earlier era, one that anyone who has ever listened to Lawrence Welk would recognize. So to listen to him speaking, especially in Singapore, at the Singapore American School, no less, seemed a bit out of place, both geographically and professionally. But make no mistake, he would prove to be a magnificent choice for that job. When Bob talked to you, you were the center of his universe. He looked you in the eye and you could see the concentration and pure interest in your words. And if you didn't see him for months, he remembered every detail about you, your family, anything that came out of that first encounter. This is one of his many gifts, that all who encountered the man noticed. He truly is relationship-driven, to his core.

On my next home leave after Bob was hired, I told a cousin about Bob, who immediately turned thoughtful. I could see the wheels turning. He said, "Bob Gross....I think Bob's grandfather was Rafeal, and I know that Rafeal was your Dad's Mother's First Cousin."

Which prompted me to ask him: "Do you know the entire family tree of the state of North Dakota?"

Upon return to Singapore, I happened to be at a dinner function with Superintendent Gross in attendance. I wandered over to his table and asked, "Bob, is your grandfather Rafeal?"

He looked at me, a bit puzzled, before answering, "Yes."

I replied, "Well, hello, cuz!"

In true North Dakota fashion, his next words were, "I knew you were from good stock."

Rod Jahner, Wake Forest, North Carolina

13.

To and From Sweden with Love

Some Fargo wisdom from abroad.

I come from Poland originally; I've never been to Fargo, not even to the U.S. But I know a person, who's been my friend for more than 15 years, who's a wonderful Fargo ambassador abroad. Joy lives close to Fargo, and has an amazing way to show her kindness.

I was left speechless when I saw her at my door in August of 2008, knowing that she was supposed to be in Scotland or on her way back to the U.S. Instead, she chose to make a huge surprise for me by visiting me and my newborn baby. She chose to buy a flight to Stockholm, where I live, and fly home from here instead. She stayed for just one day, making it even more amazing that she put herself to so much trouble and expense just to see us for such a short while.

Not to mention her handmade patchwork fleece blanket, which we got one week before our son was born. She must've spent weeks making it, although she was working at two places at the time, having so little time for herself.

Those are some of my best experiences, both coming from somebody living close to you.

I want to speak about some other people as well. "Fargo" people exist everywhere.

I will never forget my first visit to Iran in 2003. We were driving with my husband through some rural area. Suddenly we saw a field full of grapes and an older couple picking them up. We stopped and asked them if we could buy their grapes, they looked delicious. They agreed and helped us to fill the bag, which soon became full. When we wanted to pay, the woman handed over another, equally full bag and told us we didn't need to pay, that God would pay them one day for feeding travelers. We tried our best to convince them and pay for this generous gift, but in vain. They were equally firm as they were kind and warm-hearted.

Maybe those people are not the first we hear about on the news channels, but they are around us and they make us want to be much better human beings. Let's hope we and our children will keep meeting them.

Magdalena Kodura, Sweden

Book IV

True Fargo Crime

You can learn a lot about a place from its Dark Side.

1.

True Fargo Crime

Looking at Fargo from the other direction.

Over the last three years, I've seen, heard or received very few stories about crime in the Fargo region. Not enough to write much about.

But of course, every time I read or watch or listen to the local news, I usually take in something about local crime. *Usually.* Now there's something I never could have said anywhere else I've ever lived, where crime *always* predominated the local newscasts. But as you'll see, crime almost *never* predominates the news here. Sometimes, there are just no significant crimes to report.

Truth be told, crime gave my wife and I our first clue how different Fargo was, the first night we spent in town. You can learn a lot from the Dark Side of anything. You'll read that story next.

But here's the real reason I wrote **Book IV: True Fargo Crime:** I had a question of my own about the nature of crime here that I wanted to look into. So I decided to do some investigating, and take you along with me. I wrote the following pages in real time as I was conducting my investigation. I didn't know what I was going to find, and how it was all going to turn out, until the very end.

So this is a bit different from the previous three Books of Close Encounters. It's my personal look into the nature of crime in our region, interspersed with some true, mostly recent stories.

2.

The Night of the Graffiti

Our first Close Encounter with Fargo Crime.

It was a little after 9 p.m., late June, 2001. Charlene, the kids and I had flown up from Phoenix to Minneapolis earlier in the day, then driven a rental car the 250-plus miles northwest up I-94 to Fargo. We'd arrived at "Aunt Melody's" house late afternoon and spent a couple of hours catching up and eating dinner. It was our first night in Fargo. We were on vacation.

The kids were in the basement watching a Disney video. Melody was off in another part of the house doing something, and Charlene and I were sitting together on the living room couch watching television. After a full day and a little over 1,500 miles of travel, we were zoning. Eyelids heavy. I have no recollection of the show we were watching.

But I remember the 15-second news tease that popped up during a commercial break at about 9:30 p.m. Like it was yesterday.

"Coming up on WDAY: Three teenage boys have been taken into custody in connection with the graffiti found on the south wall of the gym of West Fargo High School last week. Details at ten."

My jaw dropped. I couldn't believe what I'd just heard. I looked over at Charlene, wide-eyed: "Are you telling me that's their top story?"

"I know!" Charlene giggled.

I was suddenly wide awake. My mind was racing, taking in the implications. "I've never heard the words 'graffitti' and 'custody' used in the same sentence before!"

"I *know*!" Charlene said again, still giggling.

"That's their biggest news?"

"Reminds me of growing up in Neillsville," Charlene said, referring to her girlhood home, a small town in the middle of rural Wisconsin – about 500 miles east of where we sat right that moment.

"The police actually have time to track down teenage graffitiers?" I said, still dumbstruck.

"Oh, yeah, honey, that's a big deal around here. Shhh. The show's back on."

I was looking at the TV but couldn't follow the show. My head was spinning. Graffiti? A crime? Where we lived, it was just a fact of life. "Tags" went up and came down like stoplights changing from red to green, covered up every week or two, back again every other week or two. Murders, burglaries, bank robberies – *those* were crimes. And there were enough of them that many went unsolved, forever. I had a reporter friend at the Arizona Republic, the state's largest newspaper, who'd told me there were days when five or six homicides took place in the Phoenix area, and two or three of the more "normal" ones wouldn't make it onto the news or into the paper at all. *Not a mention.* There weren't any police in Arizona with time to spend tracking teenagers who'd committed graffiti.

But wait. Maybe that news tease wasn't about the biggest crime of the day. Maybe it was just an interesting tease. If so, it worked: I was definitely going to watch the news. Fargo had a population approaching 100,000 people. Surely they had some real crime.

So at 10 p.m., I was right there, glued. Sure enough, the graffiti story was first. Seems a patch of very amateurish graffiti had shown up on the south wall of the West Fargo High gym a few days earlier, and a full-blown investigation had ensued. Newscasts had asked for anyone with information to contact the police, officers had canvassed some nearby neighborhoods, the whole shebang – considerably more of a community effort than I could remember ever seeing back in Arizona or California, for even heinous crimes. So today, three teenagers had been identified, apparently confessing right away. They were now back home without bail, catching hell from their moms and dads, no doubt.

Wow.

But wait: The second story was coming on. Maybe it would be a real crime.

Nope. It was a car accident or something. Someone broke a bone or two, was taken to the hospital, patched up and released.

Again, a story that would never make it on the news anywhere I'd ever lived or visited before.

That was the first time the thought began trickling into my brain: *What planet are we on?* I'd thought we'd just traveled fifteen hundred miles that day. But watching the first couple minutes of the local news, it felt like fifteen billion.

I was up off the couch and moving around now, slightly agitated. The third story was about a community event or some equally non-violent, non-criminal, socially constructive activity. That was all the news I could handle, that first night in Fargo.

"Mel, what's the population of Fargo?" I remember asking. My world view was being shifted, violently. I was trying to hold on to reality. I mean, you build up a world view over four-and-a-half decades, and then in about 90 seconds some small-town newscast puts a 9.0 on the Richter Scale under it. I needed something to hold on to.

234

Maybe Fargo was a lot smaller than I thought. That might explain it.

"I don't know, I think it's close to a hundred thousand now," she said. "And if you think about the whole area, you know, if you add in West Fargo and Moorhead and all the little towns – I guess you'd call them suburbs –"

Charlene laughed. "Where we come from, Fargo would be a suburb!"

"Oh, I know!" Mel was laughing, too, now.

"Yeah, Glendale's over two-hundred thousand now," I said, not laughing as much. I was still trying to get my bearings on Planet Fargo. "So what would – what would the population of the whole Fargo metro area be, about?" I asked, looking at Mel.

"Oh, I'm pretty sure it's a little over two hundred thousand now, too."

That blew my theory all to heck. The Phoenix metro area was now 3.5 million. Two hundred thousand was about 1/18th that size. But I hadn't seen 1/18th the crime on that newscast. I'd seen more like 1/1800th.

Instead of calming down, my mind was speeding up. "Do they – uh, Mel, is that like a normal newscast we just saw tonight?"

"She didn't watch the news with us, Marc," my wife explained the obvious, then turned to Mel: "He's all excited because the biggest story was about some graffiti on some gym—"

"Oh, did they catch those guys?" Mel asked.

I burst out laughing. "Yeah. Which just blows me away. I mean, you remember Glendale, Mel. If they ran around catching all the kids doing graffiti there, they'd have to commandeer one the larger high schools and covert it into a juvenile offender processing facility."

Mel and Char were chuckling. "Oh, I know," said Mel. Yeah, it's different here, you know, more small town, more Midwestern."

"Yeah, but just off the top of my head," I said, "it's not a population thing. Unless it's really weird that the biggest crime of the day is catching some teenagers who put a little graffiti on the outside of a gym."

"Actually, it was a pretty big patch," Mel said, inadvertently making my point. I started laughing.

She continued: "It was about ten by ten or something. They showed a big photo of it in the paper when it happened, with a couple of obscenities blocked out."

This is a different planet from the one I grew up on, I knew now. *These people are not the humans I have lived amongst all my life.* But I still had to re-check.

"So, what you're saying, Mel, is that it's not that unusual for the big crime story of the day to be about graffiti or something like that?"

"Well, there isn't much graffiti, so that's really unusual, but you're just asking how bad the crime is, right?"

"Right." I said.

"Well, I don't watch the news much, but we have bad crimes up here, Marc. We have murders, we usually only have about one murder a year..."

My head started spinning again. I felt like some computer on an old TV sci-fi: *Does not compute... does not compute... One murder a year? One murder a year? Two hundred thousand people? Five murders a day in Phoenix sometimes?*

Mel was still talking, back on Planet Fargo: "... but I'd say, you know, sometimes there's a break-in on the news or something, a house or a business has been robbed..."

Head... spinning... more... In Phoenix, you were lucky to get police showing up right away if you'd been robbed, much less have the media covering it...

"... but sometimes," Mel was blithely continuing along, a total innocent. She had no idea the havoc she was wreaking on my grasp of the reality of my own species at the turn of the 21st century. "...sometimes there's not any real crime on the news. That doesn't mean it didn't happen, you know, I bet the police always get a call or two about a domestic disturbance of something..."

She was still talking but I couldn't really take any more in. It was too-much-change-in-too-short-a-time. Overload. I mustered everything I had to pleasantly nod my head and say, "mmm-hmm" until she finished, then "Thanks, Mel – and thanks for having us!" Char and I gave her a hug and went to bed. I was dazed. Within seconds of lying down I was out like a light, even though, as I closed my eyes, I could feel the world spinning.

It occurs to me now for the first time, just as I write this, maybe that's what Charlene had in mind all along, when she'd decided we were going to Fargo on vacation.

God I love that woman.

3.

Number Crunching

A different planet. Definitely a different planet.

We were moving to Fargo. *This summer.* It was late June, 2005, almost exactly four years since our first encounter with Planet Fargo, and The Night of the Graffiti. I was in Arizona with the kids and my mom, selling our two places (my mom was in her eighties and we'd all decided it would be best if she moved up and in with us, too. Seemed like the Fargo thing to do.)

I started thinking about Fargo crime again, and the tiny amount of crime reportage compared to Phoenix. I found myself wondering: *Just how much lower is the Fargo crime rate?*

So one afternoon, I did a little Internet research. Between 2001 and 2004, there'd only been one homicide in Fargo! During the same period, 2001-2004, in Glendale, Arizona (the town we were leaving) there'd been 66 homicides! Glendale, though, had a population of just under 240,000 – about 2½ times the size of Fargo, at a little over 90,000. Some quick math showed that the murder rate in Glendale was a little more than 25 times that of Fargo. *No wonder the Fargo news is so damn cheery,* I thought to myself. *They hardly have anything else to report on.*

Just for fun, after writing that last paragraph I went to www.bookofodds.com to find a comparison – and found that the odds of getting murdered during any given year in Glendale between 2001 and 2004 were about five times higher than the odds of getting injured messing around with a hammock (ever mess with a hammock? I've had a few close calls, myself), whereas the odds of getting murdered in Fargo during that period were pretty close to the odds of being struck by lightning.

But that was eight years ago. Time for an update. This time, though, let's do more than crunch some numbers. I've been on this brave, happy little Fargo planet eight years now, and I'll tell you: Numbers alone don't begin to tell the story.

4.

To Protect and Serve

Man, how cool is this? What planet am I on?

"Fargo Police Department."

"Hi, I have a weird question," I said.

"Okay...?" the lady on the other end said, voice questioning but still friendly. That was good.

"My name is Marc de Celle, and I'm the author of the book *How Fargo of You...*"

"I'm reading it. You left one in the lobby. I know you."

It took me a second to put that together. Then I remembered the friendly, pretty face behind the inch-thick bulletproof glass in the lobby of the downtown Fargo police station. "Oh, are you the lady – ummm, officer, are you the officer that was there the day I left a signed copy on the little table in…"

"Yeah." Still friendly. Good.

"Oh, great! If you've read a little of my book you'll understand my weird question."

"Okay," she said, even friendlier, still patiently waiting for my weird question.

"Well, I'm writing a follow-up, and I'm writing a section on Fargo crime, because even the crime here is different…"

"Yeah…"

"And I suspect," I said, raising my tone of voice just a little for emphasis, "that the biggest story about Fargo crime since we moved here in two-thousand five…"

"Yeah?" She sounded pretty curious now. Good.

"Ummm, you know, just as a casual observer of the news, it seems to me that about half the murders since we moved here were committed by someone who hadn't yet lived here a full year."

I paused for a second. Silence on the other end. *I'd better keep going.*

"So, I want to check this out, because if it's true I think it might be the biggest story about crime in Fargo. I mean, we already have an extremely low murder rate compared to most places, and if half of them are committed by people who haven't yet lived here a full year, uhh, well, it doesn't just mean that people who grow up around here are very unlikely to kill someone. I have a theory that people who move here, like I did, if we've been here long enough, we tend to calm down enough that we're really unlikely to kill someone. I know I did…"

I suddenly realized how that sounded.

"I don't mean I was going to kill anybody…"

She laughed.

"…I just mean I just noticed that I'd calmed down a lot, you know, by the time we'd lived here a year."

"Okay…" she said, nicely.

I suddenly realized she was still waiting for my weird question. "Anyway, I want to find out if my hunch is right. So I figured out that all I need a list of the names of people who've been convicted of murder in our area since two-thousand five, the year we got here, or, even better, maybe since two-thousand, so I can write the story about the twenty-first century. Because if I have those names, I can do an Internet search on each of them, and get their background story from the press articles…"

"I think we can do that for you," She said, still very friendly, interrupting my monologue. I was grateful. "What's your phone number? I'll see if I can put that together for you and call you back."

"Awesome! Thanks, Amy."

Now you might think, if you've never spent much time in this part of the world, that Amy was being extra helpful because she knew my book. But as you'll learn in these pages, extreme helpfulness on the part of government officials is the norm here, while minor celebrity counts for next to nothing – *everyone* is considered important. And as I gave Amy my phone number, I thought back to what dealing with government officials back in Arizona and California for the first fifty years of my life had been like. *Fargo really is a different planet,* I found myself thinking yet again.

As I waited for Amy to call me back, I decided to go through my stack of Fargo stories – the hundreds people had sent me – and pull out the ones I'd marked "Crime." There were only five. I looked through them and started reading one from someone I'd met.

5.

Anonymous Deputy Mechanic

Without a lot a crimes to solve, the police don't need
a lot of help around here. But they get it, anyway.

It was my sophomore year of college, and I was heading home
to the west side of the state, to Dickinson, for Christmas break,
2004. It was mid-morning on a typical December day in the
Fargo area; not too cloudy or cold. I had packed up my car with
2-3 weeks' worth of clothes and Christmas presents for my
whole family. Before I left I needed to fill up my tank and went
to "my" gas station (ya know the one you always go to) by my
apartment. Of course being from a smaller town I was used to
leaving my keys in the ignition while I went in to pay for my

gas. Little did I know that right before I came in to pay, one of the mechanics from the body shop next door had kicked out what some might call a "questionable character" who had been loitering in the store a for awhile.

When I got up to the counter to pay, the cashier asked me which pump and I then turned around to say "the blue one on pump number thr..." but instead I saw someone sitting in my car. My honest first thought was "Oh. poor guy, accidently got into my car," but the cashier stopped this innocent thought with "Oh my gosh! That man is stealing your car!" That was the first time I truly knew what "weak in the knees" meant.

After a quick moment I found myself sitting in a chair and getting my composure back to call my mom and roommate. I was crying and probably a little hysterical. I found out later that during that time the mechanic had gotten in the store's tow truck with a CB radio and taken off after the thief, and he was talking to the police telling them where my car was heading. Of course I have no true memory of where my car was or how it was being driven, but before I knew it the cops had found and stopped the man who stole my car. Within an hour I was back in my car and was on my way home for Christmas. One thing I wish I would have done was send a card or a nice fruit basket to the mechanic. If you are that mechanic who helped me get my car back, THANK YOU.

Kathryn Steve, West Fargo

Oh, that's good, I thought, as I finished Katherine's story. *Shows how the whole community acts like one big extension of the police department. At first glace, it looks like vigilantism, but on closer inspection, you can see it's the opposite...*

6.

Attack!

Hell hath no fury like four Fargo women chasing a thief through a parking lot.

Holding Kathryn's story in my hand, I suddenly remembered a copy of *The Forum* – North Dakota's largest newspaper, based in Fargo – I'd saved from about a month earlier. I looked over the piles on my messy desk. There it was! I grabbed it. The top half of the front page was filled with a photo of a smiling, fiftyish woman standing in a parking lot, next to her car. Emblazoned above the photo:

The Forum

Friday, July 19, 2013

WOULD-BE THIEF PICKS WRONG PURSE

With three strangers' help, pastor's wife foils brazen theft

The images from that day were already flashing through my mind as I looked at the paper. I'd first heard the story on the radio, then watched it that night on the local news: The lady in the photo had set her purse on the seat of her car while she loaded up her groceries. Suddenly, a heavyset man in his twenties had just reached into her car, grabbed her purse and started running.

In typical Fargo style – the same style displayed by the quick-thinking mechanic in Kathryn's story – the middle-aged lady lunged after him, grabbing his T-shirt and running to keep up, yelling at him to give her purse back. His T-shirt began to rip completely off his back, so she grabbed a handful of his long, dark, curly hair, still hollering at him to return her purse. But just as the man started to slow, she slipped and went down.

I checked the Forum article. Pam. Her name was Pam. Pam Thompson. The article, by Forum Reporter Emily Welker, was well written, like a little thriller, and I couldn't put it down. It brought all the details from that day back into full focus.

By the time Pam fell down on the asphalt, she'd made enough of a scene that three other women in the parking lot had seen what was going on.

That was enough, in Fargo. The guy didn't have a prayer.

From the pavement of the parking lot, Pam saw two other women "taking off like shots after him," she said, "shouting at him, telling him he didn't have to do this."

Loved that part. So Fargo. Even while in attack-dog mode, these women are still trying to reason with the bad guy. Telling him, in so many words, it's not as bad as he must think it is to be doing such a crazy thing.

And it wasn't. "If he'd have asked me for money, I would have given him money," Pam said afterwards.

When the chase started, a woman driving a van through the parking lot had seen Pam ripping the shirt off the guy's back. As Pam fell, the lady in the van could see the bad guy appeared to be running toward a red car moving slowly through the parking lot. She stopped, threw her van into reverse and backed up, blocking the end of the aisle the red car was heading down, where the now-gasping bad guy, still clutching Pam's purse, was headed, the two other women in hot pursuit.

As Pam was getting up off the asphalt, the bad guy tripped and went down. He got up, leaving the purse behind him on the ground, then weaving his way through a few parked vehicles to make it to the red getaway car. But the lady in the van followed the red car as it maneuvered away – and she was able to get the license plate number.

The vehicle had been identified, the article said. But that was where it ended.

Hmmmm. I wondered if they ever caught the bad guys. I suspected they weren't from Fargo, or they would have already known what those ladies had been yelling at them: "You don't have to do this."

I did a quick Internet search for Pam Thompson, but couldn't find any articles since the one by Emily Welker. That article said Pam was married to Reverend Bill Thompson, pastor of the Lutheran Church of the Cross. I decided to give the church a call.

I looked in the yellow pages under churches. Too many Lutheran denominations. Lutheran Brethren, Lutheran ELCA, Lutheran Missouri Synod... I had no way of knowing which section to look under to find the Lutheran Church of the Cross.

Let's just try the business section of the white pages, I thought to myself. *That's better:* There was a good third of a page of Lutheran Churches. Lutheran Church of this, that and the other thing, one line after the other. All I had to find was "of the Cross." There. I dialed the number.

"Lutheran Church of the Cross," a pleasant female voice answered.

"Hi, I have kind of an odd question," I said.

"Alright, I'll do my best," the pleasant voice said, still pleasant.

"Well, I was wondering, do you know if they ever caught the bad guys who tried to steal Pam Thompson's purse last month?"

"Boy, that's a good question," the pleasant lady said. "I don't know. You know, Pam is married to our pastor, Bill Thompson. He's out right now, but I can call his cell phone and have him give you a call."

"That would be great," I said, and gave her my number.

About two minutes later, the phone rang. Caller ID said it was a cell phone. It was a number I didn't recognize, with a local area code. I guessed it was probably the Reverend.

I answered.

"Hi, Marc?"

"Yes?"

"This is Bill Thompson. I understand you have questions about my wife Pam's adventure." He had a great, warm voice. Good for happy sermons, I guessed.

"Yeah, Bill, thanks for calling me back. I was just wondering if they ever caught the bad guys. The article in the Forum said they were able to identify the red car, but that was it, and I couldn't find any follow-up articles."

"No, Marc, they haven't apprehended anyone. They traced the vehicle to a lady who lives just outside the Cities." ("The Cities" is how people in Fargo refer to the "Twin Cities" of Minneapolis and St. Paul, in the center of Minnesota, about 250 miles southeast of here.) "But she had an alibi showing she was clearly somewhere else at the time. She said her boyfriend may have taken her car, but she wasn't sure. And her boyfriend has a pretty long rap sheet. But they don't seem to be able to get past that stage – after all, they can't get a warrant to check for stolen property, since there isn't any!"

We both laughed.

"Well, Bill," I said, "that sort of answers my real question anyway, because I'd guessed that these guys probably weren't from around here."

"No," the Reverend said, "Didn't seem like they would be, and doesn't look like they were."

"Umm, do you have an email address?" I asked. "I'll want to email you a copy of the rough draft so if I've gotten anything wrong you can fix it."

"Sure, Marc..." He gave me his email address.

"Well, I appreciate your time, Bill, and please give my best wishes to Pam. You can tell her I think what she did was very Fargo."

Bill laughed. "Alright Marc, thanks. She'll appreciate that."

I suddenly remembered something. "Oh, Bill. Just one more thing."

"Yeah?"

"I got a real kick out of what your wife said at the end of the article."

"Uhh, what was that? You'll have to remind me."

"Well, when the Intrepid Reporter Emily Welker asked Pam if she'd do it all over again, if she had any regrets..."

The reverend started laughing. "Oh yeah, she risks her life going after a brazen thief in a parking lot, and she'd do that all over again – but she wishes she hadn't sworn at the guy!"

"Doesn't get any more Fargo than that!" I added, through the laughter.

After I got off the phone with the Reverend, I looked back at the four stories I had left marked "Crime." I shuffled through them, just reading the titles. One caught my attention.

7.

A Very Fargo Break In

He saw the crazy woman in her nightie, barreling down the stairs
towards him with a wheelchair leg in her hand,
and was immediately sober.

What do you tell the would-be burglar who breaks your window in the dead of night to get into your house, who then comes back the next day with a fresh pane of glass and an apology, then proceeds to install the glass and buy you a 12-pack of beer?

How TOTALLY Fargo of you!!

It was about 2 am, 2002, we were living in a rather shady area of Fargo... as ghetto as Fargo gets. I was in college and my family and I were renting a really old beautiful house on college street in North Fargo. Even though the neighborhood was run-down, the people there were as Fargo as they come. My sister lived on the same block, too. I awoke to a frantic phone call from her. Someone had tried to break into her house. She awoke to the sound of breaking glass. She quickly grabbed the closest thing to a baseball bat she could find, which was one of the footrests from her husband's wheelchair. She ran down the stairs like a crazy woman yelling obscenities, hoping it would scare the intruder away and they didn't have a gun and an itchy trigger finger. A very inebriated man was sticking his hand through the glass trying to reach the lock on her door. He saw the crazy woman in her nightie, barreling down the stairs towards him with a wheelchair leg in her hand, and was immediately sober.

He staggered down the outside stairs and ran for it. She called the police and her landlord and spent the next few hours trying to come down from the adrenalin high. The next morning, she hears a knock on the door and opens it to the very contrite face of the man who attempted to break into her house. He was there to apologize and fix her window. Apparently his friends dropped him off at what they thought was his house, he was too drunk to think any different and when he tried opening the door and it was locked, figured he had locked the keys in his house and had to break a window to get in. When he saw my sister screaming like a banshee he knew he had made a grievous error. He ran for it and eventually found his house. When he sobered up he came back to the house to fix her window that he had broken the night before. Now this guy didn't have to come back, he was in the clear! But he did... how very Fargo of him!

Diana Lang, Fargo

Now that's a Fargo criminal, I thought to myself. Then the phone rang.

8.

The Deputy Chief of Police

"It's Claus, just like Santa." How appropriate.

The caller ID read **Fargo Police**.

"Hello?" I answered.

"Hi, Marc?"

"Yeah, I'm him."

"Hi. Marc, Deputy Chief Pat Claus. I understand you have a question…"

Whoa. *Deputy Chief.* I guess Amy couldn't put together the list for me herself.

"Yeah, uhmm, did Amy talk to you?"

"Yes, she did."

"Well, Umm, I'm the author of *How Fargo of You*. Are you familiar with the book?"

"Yes," he said in a happy tone, "I am." *Oh, good.*

"Well, I'm writing my follow-up, and it has a section on Fargo crime, because I think it's pretty different, in some ways-"

"Yeah."

"And I..."

Well, this is where I explained to him what I told Amy earlier, about what I thought the biggest story about Fargo crime might be, and why I needed the list of names. You don't really want to read that same schpeel all over again, do you? No.

So after I finished my explanation of what I was looking for and why, Deputy Chief Claus said, "Well, Marc, there are certain requests for information made by the public that we're required by law to fill, and this isn't one of those, but we can do it for you. I mean, it's not a long list, we average about one murder a year, so if we go back to two-thousand-and-one, that's about thirteen names. But first, I have a question –"

"Yeah?"

"What area are you interested in? Because by law, we can only give you the records from the City of Fargo. So we won't be able to give you the names of anyone convicted of murder in West Fargo, or other cities in the metro area." I knew West Fargo was one of the fastest-growing cities in the entire U.S., with a population nearing 30,000 – nearly double what it was in 2000. It's physically conjoined with Fargo. I immediately realized the Deputy Chief had a valid point: It wouldn't be a valid test of my theory – the idea that people who live here for more than a year are a lot less likely to commit murder – if I didn't include West Fargo.

"Oh. No, I should get the names from a wider area." I said.

"Yeah, that's what I thought. So I'll tell you what to do. Go see the Clerk of the Court for Cass County. They've got a computer there with all those records, and it will have the names of everyone convicted of any murder that's taken place in the county, and it will show where the murder took place, and all the other details."

"Oh, good."

"I don't know what's involved in getting them to share that with you, but it's public record, so it shouldn't be too hard."

"Well, thanks very much, Pat," I said. "I really appreciate your help."

"No problem. If you need any more help, feel free to call me back, Marc. It's Deputy Chief Pat Claus. Claus, just like Santa."

We both laughed. *How appropriate*, I thought to myself, *with all they give us.*

But I didn't know the half of it. Yet.

9.

Can the Police Be Too Helpful?

Well, when they figure out it's sort of a violation of the law, yes.

I suddenly remembered something.

"...Oh, Pat. One more thing. I've got another question for you, if you've got time. Do you have a few more minutes?"

"Sure, Marc, what is it?"

"Well, our first visit here was in the summer of two-thousand one, and my first interaction with Fargo was at the Petro station at forty-fifth street and I-ninety four."

"Yeah?"

"So, that was before Fargo had any card readers on the pumps, and I remember wondering why they didn't have any card readers yet, because we'd had them in Arizona for a few years already at that time. There was just a big sign that said 'Please Pay Inside,' so I walked in and handed my credit card to a perky twentysomething girl standing behind that huge gas console they have there, and I told her I needed to fill up on pump ten. And she looked down at the console, and her brow kind of furrowed, and she said, 'But you haven't pumped yet.'"

Pat chuckled. *Oh good,* I thought to myself. *He gets it.*

"Well, you could have knocked me over with a feather."

He chuckled again. I'd told this story hundreds of times – the story of my first face-to-face encounter with living, breathing Fargo – I'd told it before we moved here, I'd told it before I'd written **How Fargo of You**, and since then I'd told it to a hundred different groups in a hundred different settings – and every time, I relived the amazement of that moment, the discovery of a modern, 21st century world I hadn't previously believed possible. And the chuckles of the Deputy Chief of the Fargo Police Department were all the encouragement I needed to dive in again.

"You know, Pat, in that first interaction with Fargo, at that moment, I sort of felt myself being lifted out of the world I'd known all my adult life. I was almost dizzy. Images from my previous four-and-a-half decades started flashing before my eyes."

Another chuckle. *Excellent.*

"I couldn't remember anything like this ever happening before, where I was anonymously assumed to be a decent person in a business transaction with someplace I'd never set foot in before. So I looked at that young lady holding my credit card and asked, 'You mean you want me to fill up... and *then* pay you?'"

"And she got this smile of recognition on her face, you know, because that gas station is right on the Interstate – "

"Yeah," Pat chimed in, still chuckling.

" – so this probably happened to her all the time, you know, I could see a twinkle in her eye that sort of said, *'Oh, good, we've got a newbie...'*"

The Deputy Chief of Police was laughing, now, not just chuckling. This encouraged me immensely.

"I mean, this was clearly her favorite part of her job, you know, as she handed my credit card back to me, she almost sang her next lines, like she was in a Rogers and Hammerstein musical: 'Yeah, that's right, just go fill up and then come baaa--ck and we'll take caaa---re of you!'"

Another good laugh.

"And so, I can remember thinking, when I got back out to the pump, and the hair sort of stood up on the back of my neck, and I was thinking, "This must be what community feels like." And later, I realized that was why they didn't have card readers on their pumps yet, even though we'd had them in Arizona and California for years, because why did they need them? I mean, I'm sure it must cost a few hundred thousand to change out all the pumps in a truck stop that big, you know, buying and installing all those new pumps with card readers, and if you're not worried about people driving off, why spend all that money?"

"Yeah, you've got a point," the Deputy Chief chimed back in, his laughter subsiding. I wondered if he suspected where I was heading with all this. I was pretty sure he did.

"So that was my introduction to Fargo, Pat, except for having watched the news the night before with my wife, and the big crime story had been about apprehending three teenagers who'd graffitied a wall on the outside of a school gym earlier in the week, you know, and where we lived at the time, in Arizona, well, I had a reporter friend who told me there were some days when there were six or seven homicides in Phoenix, and two or three of the more 'normal' ones wouldn't even make it onto the news."

"Yeah, we're pretty lucky to live here, aren't we?" Pat said.

"Yeah, well, thanks in large part to the great work you guys do, Pat, you know, in less than twenty-four hours after arriving here, we were starting to realize we had entered a pretty different world from the one we knew, but – " I paused, thinking about exactly what I wanted to say next.

"Yeah?" *Still friendly, but maybe a little anxious, too.*

"Sorry I'm taking so long to get to my question – "

"Oh, no, Marc, I've been enjoying it." A little chuckle.

"Well, good, Pat, I appreciate your patience, and, uh, what I've been leading up to is that a couple of years ago, I think it was 2011, not long after my book came out, I remember pretty vividly when the story that the Petro was no longer going to continue their 'Pump first, then Pay Policy' hit the news. And, I mean, of course by that time they had card readers, everyone had them by that time, if only because customers expected the convenience of not having to go inside to pay. So I knew that must be part of it. But by that time, I knew the lady, Diane, who owned the Petro, because they were selling a ton of my books. So the next time I went in to see her, I asked her why she'd changed the policy, was it because of all the people coming in from out of state heading to the oil boom, and she was getting too many drive-offs? And she said, no, it was because the Fargo Police Department was no longer tracking down the drive-offs like they used to, they'd stopped doing that, but up in Minot, right in the middle of the oil boom, she told me, she owned another gas station where they still had 'Pump and Pay,' because the police there still tracked down drive offs. So ever since then I've wanted to talk to the Police Chief about that change and find out why it happened, and, I know you're not the Chief, but since I had you here on the line already, I thought I'd ask you."

"Well, Marc, I'm really glad you asked me," he said, sounding genuinely glad – "because I'm the guy who made that change. When I got this position, I discovered we had a whole little operation where a gas station owner would call in with a license plate number and we'd tell them the address the car was registered to, and sometimes, we'd even send a patrol car out to the place. And most of the time, the people would say, "Oh, I'm sorry, I must have forgotten to pay, and they'd just pay, and there had even been a few instances where the officer took the money to the gas station –"

I was laughing so hard he had to pause for a second. "Oh my God," I said, "That is so *Fargo!*"

"You're right!" he agreed. "And in almost all these cases, there would be no charges filed. But it was quite a little operation we had set up, and a fair chunk of department time and resources were going into it. When I checked into it, I found out that what we were doing was actually against the law. First of all, we're not bill collectors, we're paid by the public's dollars to enforce the law and ensure public safety, and we shouldn't be spending the public's money to help a business do collections, and if we're doing bill collecting for one industry, but not others, that's probably grounds for something, too. And also, we didn't really know who we were giving this information to, I mean they'd call up and say they'd had a drive-off, and here was the license plate number, but maybe it was just some guy who wanted to know the address of a cute girl he'd seen getting gas. We had no way of knowing."

"Yeah, I get it." It made a lot of sense.

"I'm sure it all started years ago, when Fargo was a lot smaller, and some gas station owner called up a guy he knew in records or something, 'Oh sure, Joe, I can get that for you...'. But now, it was just whoever was working at a gas station, and we didn't really have any way of even knowing that. So the way it was being done, there was no way of verifying any of it was valid police business, but it was clear that almost none of it was. We already knew that because charges were almost never filed."

"I get it," I said again, "and I bet the number of accidental drive offs would have really gone up after card readers went in place, because it would be so much easier to absent-mindedly drive off! I mean, if you have to walk inside to pay, it's hard to forget you haven't done that. But if all you do is slide your card, and if the pumps work even if you don't slide your card – never the case in Phoenix or L.A., I assure you, none of those pumps worked before your card was approved – anyway, I can see how card readers would make it a lot easier to absent mindedly drive off without paying." I suddenly found myself wondering if I'd ever done it! Too busy thinking about my writing, not my gas pumping… certainly could happen… Maybe I was a fugitive and didn't know it! Talking to the Deputy Chief of Police about the very crime I didn't even realize I'd committed…

"Well, you might be right about that, Marc, but when I became Deputy Chief almost every place had readers, so I didn't get to watch the changeover and see if the number of drive-offs went up at that time, but they very well might have, I wouldn't be surprised if you're right.

"Anyway," the Deputy Chief returned to his story, "so after I figured out what was going on, I told the Chief about it, and I figured out how it could all be done the right way. So we sent a letter out to all the gas station owners. First, if they just wanted to get the address the license plate was registered to, they would have to send a letter to the DMV in Bismarck (the capital of

North Dakota) requesting that information. They actually have a form for those requests, where the person making the request has to attest to who they are, that kind of thing, so it's actually legal for the DMV to give that information out. And it takes a few days and costs three dollars, but that's the lawful way for a member of the public to find out the address associated with a vehicle license number."

"But if the gas station owner wanted us to track someone down, we'd get the address, they wouldn't have to contact DMV. But they'd have to fill out a form saying why they thought this was a deliberate act, and include any video they had of the incident, because you know, if you see people filling up with hoodies covering their faces and then driving off, well, you figure it probably was intentional and that video is important evidence. And the gas station owner would have to sign the form before we'd become engaged, and the form said they were willing to press charges."

"Oh," I said, "and I bet almost none of them are ever willing to sign that form, because they don't want to press charges unless they're absolutely certain it was a real bad guy."

"That's right," the Deputy Chief of Police of Fargo confirmed. "They're too Fargo."

I laughed loudly. "Well, Pat," I said, still laughing, "thanks for the explanation – "

"Sure, Marc, I tell people, if you want too much information, just ask me. I tend to give really long explanations, but I'd rather you knew too much than get the wrong idea because I haven't told you enough."

"Well, that's one thing we have in common, Pat. How Fargo of you!"

We both laughed, and said goodbye.

10.

The Helpfulness of Fargo Officialdom

Where I come from, people are supposed to prevent access,
not facilitate it.

I called the Clerk of the Court for Cass County. Cass is the county Fargo is located in. I left a voice mail. Then, still looking at the same government pages of the phone book, I saw a listing for the "State's Attorney" of Cass County. *Wait a minute*, I realized, *I know that guy*. Birch Burdick! His father had been a U.S. Senator from North Dakota, Quentin Burdick. I'd met him at a couple of social events in town – in a place the size of Fargo, it's hard not to meet everyone.

I looked closer at the listing. Under "State's Attorney" I saw a listing for "Criminal Division." I dialed it.

"State's Attorney's office," a nice lady's voice answered.

I didn't ask for Birch, or mention that I knew him. I just told her the story, as I had Amy and Pat at the Fargo Police Department, about the list of convicted murderers I was looking for.

"Well," she said, voice still very friendly, "would you like to speak to the State's Attorney?" That was not a question I expected to hear. Where I come from, people in her position are supposed to prevent access, not facilitate it.

"Sure, I know Birch," I said. "Love to talk to him."

"Let me see if he's in," she said, and put me on hold. I looked at the clock. *Ooops.* It was 12:30. Hadn't noticed the time. Birch was probably at lunch.

She came back on the line, "Birch is out. I'll have him call you when he gets back. What's your number, Marc?"

I gave it to her and we said goodbye. Nothing to do but wait. Time for lunch.

The phone rang. I looked at the caller ID. It read CASS COUNTY. I picked it up and pushed the TALK button. I decided to save whoever it was the trouble of asking who they were talking to: "Marc de Celle."

"Hi Marc, Birch Burdick." Friendly voice. Very Fargo.

"Hi Birch, thanks for calling."

"Sure, Marc. What can I do for you?"

I explained the list I was looking for and why.

"Well, you might want a better list than I can give you, Marc. Mine will only include people convicted of a crime in Cass County. So everything in Moorhead will be missing, as well as crimes that took place in other counties, even if they were committed by people from our area."

"Yeah," I sighed, "I know, Birch. But I at least want to start with your list."

"Well, I could practically give you that list off the top of my head," Birch said, "we've only had about a dozen murders since two-thousand. But let me ask my secretary to make an actual list for you, directly off the public record."

"That'd be great, Birch, thanks."

"How would you like to receive it?"

"Email'd be great."

"Okay, Marc, what's your email address?"

I gave it to him, thanked him again, and we said goodbye.

11.

Secret Fargo Stories

A different planet. Definitely a different planet.

During lunch, while I was waiting for the call from Birch, I thought about my conversation with Deputy Chief Claus. It occurred to me that the clerks at the Stop-and-Go convenience store near my house, where I frequently pick up a soft drink or a snack, often asked, "Did you get any gas out there?" So they must still be following a pump-then-pay policy, even with all the complications from card readers and Fargo having become too big for the police department to run around collecting on accidental drive-offs.

And I thought about my Secret Fargo Stories.

These are stories I hadn't included in the book *How Fargo of You*, because I thought they might attract criminals. Not that petty thieves tend to do a lot of reading. But why invite trouble? So I'd told these stories on the radio, or on television, or to live audiences, just in Fargo, because everyone here has already seen and heard about these kinds of things a hundred times. But these stories could give people in Arizona or Florida or New York – especially anyone with criminal tendencies – the wrong idea: *Whoa, what a bunch of chumps*, I can hear a little two-bit car thief in Tucson, or Tampa Bay, or Schenectady thinking. *Fargo's easy pickins!* And his next pilfered ride wouldn't be going to the local chop shop, but heading our way.

So I'd decided not to write these stories. They were Fargo's little secrets.

But now, I began to think differently. My conversation with the Deputy Chief made me look at these stories in a new light. *If I'm going to write a whole section on True Crime in Fargo, I realized, I can put these stories in context: The truth is, Fargo is undoubtedly one of the worst places in the world for a criminal. First, almost everyone helps their fellow citizens and, by extension, when a crime happens, they help the police. There are so many people around here like the mechanic who followed Kathryn's stolen car, or Pam and the other ladies in the grocery store parking lot, a criminal is literally surrounded by relatively fearless enemies at all times. Second, the police here aren't backlogged with piles of unsolved crimes. So when a crime happens, there are lots of police with lots of time, along with all the aforementioned concerned citizens, all over the criminals, like tough-as-heck North Dakota flies on deer droppings. Third, the police almost all grew up around here, which means they not only got a great education, they also have tons of community connections – and the low crime rate allows lots of time for extra training. So when they do spring into action, it's like a fine-tuned bear trap snapping shut.*

And besides, I realized, if I leave a few critical details out of these stories, the places and businesses involved will remain completely anonymous...

So – are you ready for a secret?

12.

Lock It or Lose It

Secret Fargo Story #1.

It was a very cold evening. Up here, "very cold" means twenty below, if you include wind chill. I was driving to an undisclosed location in Fargo. As I neared the parking lot, a public service announcement came on the radio, from the Fargo Police:

"Lock it or lose it! Remember: Never leave valuables lying on the seat of your car when you park it, always take your keys and lock your car behind you. A message from the Fargo Police."

I was pulling into the parking lot now, where I saw about fifty or sixty cars – half of which had been left running, to keep them warm, with no one inside! I just started laughing.

I parked my van and locked it. I wasn't going to be inside long, so my van wouldn't get too cold, and besides, I'm not from here, so I still can't bring myself to not lock my vehicle.

I could tell most of the vehicles with their engines running weren't late models, the kind you can turn on and off from a distance with a key fob. But I just had to see with my own eyes. So, as I walked inside, I walked by a few driver's-side windows and, trying not to look too suspicious, glanced down. Sure enough! The doors were unlocked and the keys were in the ignition!

When I got inside, I looked around at these people. These amazing people. There wasn't a hint of concern. The prevailing attitude seemed to be, "Hey, if anyone needs a car that bad in this weather…"

I actually got a little misty eyed looking around the room. I can get a little sappy when it comes to Fargo. I mean, this stuff is actually real! It actually happens here! My brain circuitry was developed over fifty years in California and Arizona, so I seem unable to accept this fully. When I see stuff like this, it gets automatically filed in the part of my head that handles "make believe," "fake" and "dream on, sucker." So when I'm confronted with these realities I try not to gape openly. I have to make a conscious effort to grasp that this is reality, and whenever that connection starts to happen, even just a little, I get a little choked up.

It occurs to me, as I write this, that there's another story someone sent me that might help illustrate, just a little, where this kind of behavior comes from.

I'll go look for it.

13.

Only in North Dakota

Secret Fargo Story #2.

Editor's warning to any criminal reading this (hard to imagine,
but just in case): *This story is about a little town about an hour*
outside of Fargo, population less than 500. It's like a lot of little towns
around here. But before you read it and get all excited, I want you to
know a few facts first. First, virtually every farmer in North Dakota,
and most of the other men and many of the women, own rifles, and
have eaten things shot by them. They have skills. This also seems to be
the case with a great number of the residents of the bigger towns, too,
like Fargo. So if you have any criminal tendencies, don't start

salivating as you read this. North Dakota would probably be your worst nightmare.

My first trip to North Dakota, I knew I had stepped back in time – to a place that was like my home town in Ohio back in the 1950s. My girlfriend and future wife, Elaine, and her mother picked me up at the International Airport in Fargo. Then we drove to their house in [undisclosed location], North Dakota. After we got out of the car, I remarked that Elaine's mom had left her keys in the car. I was told that was what *everyone* did, all the time, even in town! Otherwise, they would probably all lose their keys! Also, my future father-in-law kept all his tools and equipment for his job in a garage which was kept closed with a hasp and padlock. But of course, the padlock was never closed, because if it had been, he would have needed a bolt cutter to get into the garage – he had no key for the lock! Almost every yard in town had a nice bicycle parked in it, which no one ever worried about, because no one ever took anything that wasn't theirs. No one in town locked the front door because – again – no one had a key to the door!

Only in North Dakota!

On my first trip into town, I was amazed at how W I D E the main street was – as well as the fact that it was one of the few streets that was paved! Elaine informed me that the street was so wide because that was where they pushed all the snow in the winter so that people could still "head in" park when they came to town! Main Street in [name of town] is still one of the widest streets I have ever seen, anywhere.

Only in North Dakota!

The "traffic" on Main Street consisted of two elderly women crossing the street and one old dog laying in the middle of the street. All these years later, the "traffic" hasn't gotten much worse!

Only in North Dakota!

On a later visit one year, I was driving into town when I saw a train approaching the grain elevators at the edge of [name of town]. I didn't want to attempt to beat the train to the crossing, so I slowed down a little. But I noticed that the train was also slowing, apparently to stop at the elevator and load some grain – which meant I could be waiting a l-o-n-g time. Oh, well. Then I noticed the train appeared to be going V E R Y slow. As I got to the crossing I realized that the train had stopped well short of the elevator, before reaching the road I was on, which puzzled me, so I looked closer. I couldn't believe what I saw – the train conductor was leaning out the window motioning me to go on through!! He had actually stopped the mile long (or longer!) train so I could get into town and not have to sit and wait while he was at the grain elevator!

Only in North Dakota!

Finally, one of the local "characters" was "Art". Art had gotten to the point where he was too old and too dangerous to be allowed to drive a car. The family took away his car keys (they just had to reach into his car to do this, of course). But that didn't stop Art for long – for some time after that, he could be seen all over town on his riding lawn mower!

Only in North Dakota!

I used to kid my wife about her hometown, but what a great place to grow up and raise a family!

Gary McCain, Ashville, Ohio

14.

"It's Pretty Safe Here."

Secret Fargo Story #3

A couple of years ago, my brother-in-law, Billy, had arranged for my son, Austen, and I, to take a tour of a fairly high-tech industrial facility in a small, northern Minnesota town.

We went to the office where the tour was scheduled to start. We walked into the front doors of a stuccoed, two-story, square business building, maybe 10,000 square feet, adjacent to the huge plant we were going to tour.

We were about an hour early, thinking we'd check in ahead of time before grabbing a quick bite to eat.

But there wasn't anyone there.

We were in the reception area. Except for the three of us, it was empty. Off to the right, there was what looked like a presentation room. Vacant. Past reception, we could see a long hallway with open doors on either side.

"Hello?" we called down the hall. "Anybody here?"

No answer.

I started down the hall. To the right were offices. To the left, a large conference room. Strangest of all, everything looked as if these spaces were full of people. Coats were on the backs of chairs, briefcases and laptops were spread out all over the place, even a few cell phones were scattered around the conference room table.

"Hellloo--- oooo," I called out again, louder this time. Billy and Austen did the same.

The silence was total.

It was like a scene from a spooky movie. You know, an alien abduction movie or a Rapture movie, or one of those Bermuda/Devil's Triangle things. Weird. Erie. It almost creeped me out.

Then it occurred to me we were in Northern Minnesota. I started laughing. "This is so Fargo," I said to Austen and Billy, shaking my head. "These people decided to go do something and just left everything here."

"Are you sure, dad?" Austen asked. "This is really weird."

"Yeah, but it's a Fargo kinda weird," Billy said.

We all started laughing.

We came to the end of the hallway, still laughing, and found a stairway. We started up. "Hellooo?" I called out again, loud enough to be heard up above.

"Hi," we heard from somewhere ahead, faint and distant. *An occupant!*

"Hi!" I yelled, "We're coming up!"

"Okay, I'll meet you," came a disembodied male voice back down the stairwell. As we reached the top of the stairs, a tall, white-haired, smiling gentleman in casual business attire (in this part of the world, that means "no coat or tie") was just arriving. "Hi, can I help you?" he asked.

"Yeah, we're just here for the tour," I said, taking the last step up, just ahead of Austen and Billy. "We came early, uhh, we were just going to make sure we had the times right, then grab a quick bite someplace nearby – but nobody's down there!"

"Yeah," he said, "they decided to take a visiting conference group on a quick tour of the facilities. Sort of spur-of-the-moment." He held out his hand. "Hi, I'm Mike. I'm the Director of Hospitality."

He shook my hand, then Billy's and Austen's. I looked around. The second floor was spacious and open, just a few window offices scattered around.

"There's laptops and stuff down there," Austen told Mike, "all over the place, and no one's watching them."

"Yeah, we don't worry about it," Mike replied. "It's pretty safe here."

Billy was looking at some large, framed photos of the plant hanging on the walls, taken when it was under construction. "Feel free to look around," Mike said to us.

"Cool, thanks," said Billy. Then: "Hey, Austen. Check this out." Austen walked over.

"You can come to my office if you'd like," Mike said to me, arm outstretched toward a glass-walled office, beautifully framed in light cherrywood.

"So – hospitality?" I asked as we were walking in. Is that what this building is?"

"Yeah. We have lots of visitors."

"Well, I couldn't help but laugh when I saw everybody'd just left their stuff all over the place down there," I said, shaking my head again As I sat down. "I'm not from around here, so I'm always amazed."

"Yeah, we've never had anything taken," Mike said, smiling. "Where you from, Marc?"

"I lived in Arizona and California all my life until just a few years ago," I said. "We live in Fargo now, but – "

"Good move," Mike interjected with a grin.

I laughed. "Yeah, it was," I said, nodding toward Austen. "That's my son. He and our daughter were getting close to their teenage years, and – "

"No place on earth better to grow up," Mike said.

"I think you may be right," I nodded. "And speaking of teenagers, I need to feed that one."

Mike looked at his watch. "Well, the tour starts in about forty-five minutes," he said, so you should probably go to Annie's, just across the street," he said, getting up from behind his open, table-like desk. "You can just walk there, it's about a minute away. Here, I'll point it out to you," he said, walking outside his office and over to a window above the street. "Right there." He was pointing to a storefront about twenty yards down and across the street. "You'll like it. It's good, fast, and not too expensive."

By this time, Billy and Austen had joined us. "Well, we'd better get going," Billy said. Then he looked at Mike: "Hey, thanks a lot for your hospitality!"

We all laughed. "Hey, it's what I do," Mike said.

We enjoyed lunch, and the tour. But it was the open offices, with the tens of thousands of dollars' worth of stuff just lying around, that was a Close Encounter of the Fargo Kind.

Marc de Celle

15.

Checking the News

Let's see what crimes happened today.

It was getting late in the afternoon of Monday, August 26, my first day of putting this part of the book together. I hadn't started writing anything yet, but I could already tell. *People who've never been here aren't going to believe this,* I realized. *They're just going to think I cherry-picked a bunch of stuff to make Fargo look like a fairy tale.*

Hmmm. *I need to sit down and watch the TV news, and make a note or two on every story. That will give some perspective.* So just before 5 p.m., I was there, in front of the television, pen and paper in hand, ready.

The crime stories of the day are usually pretty early in the newscast. After that, it's mostly weather, sports and community events. So when the 5 p.m. broadcast began, I was ready to write:

Opening Story: Blistering heat – the heat index (factoring in humidity) is over 100 degrees in a lot of places from South Dakota up to Canada.

Next story: Five Fargo-area schools that don't have air conditioning will be closed this week through Wednesday due to the heat. The coolest classrooms in these schools were already 85 degrees before noon. The Fargo Schools Superintendent says this is the first time Fargo Schools have ever been closed this long for heat. (It's happened for blizzards before!) He doesn't like doing it, "But the safety of the kids has to be our first concern."

Third story: Area crops are at a critical stage due to heat, not enough rain – video of a farmer showing cracks in his soil more than a foot deep.

Fourth story: Bizarre crash – a big truck in town crashed through a fence, ran up over the top of three parked cars, one guy was taking a break from work in one of the cars, but he was extricated and taken to a hospital and seems to be OK. Cause of the crash is unknown. Video from the scene is weird, shows a big rig up on top of a bunch of crushed cars in a parking lot, angled upward like it's about to take off.

Fifth story: There was another accident right in front of that bizarre crash due to some other drivers 'rubbernecking' at the weird scene.

Sixth story: A confused deer ran into Trinity Lutheran Church at 11 am this morning and broke a bunch of windows and other things in the offices trying to escape. Video shows a broken window over a desk, then a young buck in the courtyard bleeding at the mouth from injuries. It was tranquilized and removed.

Seventh story: NDSU (North Dakota State University) welcomes new students. Video looks like a little parade on campus.

Okay, that's weird, I started thinking to myself. *Usually there's a crime story by now. A car got broken into, or a shop was burgled or something. The kind of thing you'd have trouble getting the police to show up for quickly back in Arizona or California, much less the press.* But I couldn't ponder for long. I had to keep scribbling down what was coming over the newscast:

Eighth story: The Red River Regional Marksmanship Center broke ground today on a new underground rifle range. They raised $700K to build it from members and others. Advantage will be it will be quiet outside. Others will be able to use it besides members. They hope it will be open by the beginning of next year.

Ninth story: "The Bridal Shop" on 13th Avenue is apparently closing and a lot of brides are in a panic as their orders haven't been filled yet and the shop has fallen behind on their orders. The station contacted the store about these problems and they said they're offering full refunds or the option of placing their orders with other area retailers who can fill them.

Tenth story: Time for the weather. There's a severe thunderstorm watch from west of Fargo all the way to Lake Superior on the other side of Minnesota.

Eleventh story: A national story about a new app called the "Boyfriend tracker" which you can surreptitiously place on someone else's cell phone and track their movements.

Twelfth story: Tips on keeping cool in the heat.

The newscast was over. Not one crime story in the entire newscast. *Great,* I thought. *Now people who've never been here will think we just ignore crime.*

I changed the channel to watch the 5:30 p.m. local news on a different station. The opening stories were the same, although the coverage on the bizarre accident with the big rig was a lot better. They interviewed an eyewitness who saw it all happen, who said the driver of the big rig didn't try to stop, just left the road and plowed through the parking lot fence at full speed and up onto the parked cars, lifting the tires of the cab off the ground, which is what finally stopped him. There were severed power lines, the engine of the big rig was still running, wheels still turning, there was a rupture in the fuel tank and fuel was spilling out, and the driver in the big rig was unconscious – probably went unconscious before the accident, the witness speculated, based on what he'd seen. It had been a very scary scene, but the fire department rescue squad was there within a couple of minutes and got everything under control, including freeing the guy who'd been sitting in one of the cars that was run over.

This station also said the deer that had injured itself in Trinity Lutheran Church had later been put down.

This station, WDAY, which was the first television station in Fargo, is celebrating its 60th anniversary on the air with a series titled "60 at 60" – the sixty biggest stories of the last sixty years. Tonight's story is about the meth-amphetamine epidemic that hit North Dakota and Minnesota in the late '90s and early 2000s, and the huge community effort to beat it back. This all took place just before we moved here in 2005, so I'm fascinated – there's been almost no meth problems since we arrived, so how did they beat it? The story says the effort went well beyond standard police work, including workshops for citizens on how to fight the epidemic and lots of other outreach to schools, churches and other groups. For a few years, though, 90 percent of all drug cases in the region were meth cases – in 2004, just one year before we moved here, there were more than 2,000 meth busts in the region! I'd had no idea! But then a rash of laws were passed making it virtually impossible for any unregulated business to buy any of the ingredients needed to make meth except in very small quantities – and by 2006, there were less than 200 meth busts, and they've continued to drop every year ever since.

Finally! I've got news coverage having to do with crime! Not just a crime, but a crime epidemic! Well, okay, a crime epidemic from a decade ago, and it's a story about how the community pulled together and beat the epidemic, but at least it shows we have some crime!

Alright, I can already hear you readers in L.A. or Houston or D.C. saying, "That's not a crime epidemic! That was just a few hicks in the sticks with meth labs like in 'Breaking Bad.'"

Actually, it might be the definitive story in this section on Fargo crime. I can remember Phoenix struggling to beat back drug epidemics and never really succeeding. But here, just like in the flood fighting efforts, everyone and everything came together, and as a result, the community won.

The rest of the newscast was weather and sports.

Except at the very end of the newscast. They did a little human interest story about the new freshman class at Concordia College doing "Public Service Day" by cleaning up all the local Red Cross equipment.

Hey wait a minute! There's my daughter cleaning out an ambulance on television!

That's just too weird. I almost never watch a local newscast at this time of day – and now, I'm doing it for something I'm writing, and my daughter, who just moved out of the house to start college three days ago, shows up at the end of the news!

Her image is the last one shown, ending the newscast. People will never believe this if I write it.

But I can't help it. That's what happened. And if you're from around here, you know it's not that weird, because you've seen lots of friends and family on television in the past – hey, when you live in a community-oriented metro area of about 200,000, where most people are out doing something in the community most of the time and the local newscasts don't have much crime to cover, where the people in authority try to avoid the spotlight rather than hoard it, and the local news people try to cover *everything* that's going on in the community – that's what happens.

I guess we're always striving for Zero Degrees of Separation around here. And if you want to know why the crime rate is so low, maybe you don't need to look much further than that.

16.

When in Fargo

Not an indifferent planet. A different planet.

This one wasn't really a story. It was more like an email tip:

> I'm one of many Fargo-born and raised transplants to the Twin
> Cities. I absolutely loved your book, **How Fargo of You**,
> about a wonderfully unique area of the U.S.
>
> In your next book, you might wish to tell the story of the very
> responsible Fargoans who blew the whistle on the three
> drunken airline pilots openly imbibing into the early morning
> hours at the local "Speak Easy" bar. The concerned citizens
> contacted the FAA and the Northwest pilots were arrested in

Minneapolis. Criminal charges were filed and all three were
sentenced to jail.

Fargoans caring enough to do the right thing! Bravo!

Ann Kapaun

And later, I'd written Ann back:

Ann,

Thanks for the compliments!

Sorry I took so long to write back to you – How unFargo of me!
– and thanks for the great story tip! I think I remember that
story... how many years ago do you think that was?

Thanks again, Ann!

Marc

And she'd responded:

The flight took place on March 8, 1990. Captain Joseph Balzer
has written a book that tells his life story.

Good luck on your new book!

Ann

After reading this exchange, I did an Internet search on "Captain
Joseph Balzer," and found he'd written a book, *Flying Drunk*,

about his life story: Turns out, he'd been flying drunk for quite a few years before he tried doing it in Fargo. But just as Ann said, the people who saw him getting drunk with his fellow pilots in Fargo had immediately called the local offices of the FAA. Had the FAA acted faster, the three would have been arrested before flying 91 passengers on a Northwest flight from Fargo to Minneapolis later that morning. As it turned out, the flight went fine – but all three pilots received blood tests after landing, and all three were legally drunk. They were quickly fired by Northwest and convicted by the government, sentenced to jail time. I seem to remember the airline industry putting in place policies to prevent this kind of thing from happening in the future.

Since then, Balzer has done tremendous work to redeem himself, remaining sober for the last two decades and eventually becoming a Captain with American Airlines. He travels the country to speak to pilots and others about the dangers of addiction.

But I wonder how the story might have ended, had he and the other two pilots been allowed to continue to risk the lives of hundreds of passengers every week?

17.

A Fargo Kind of Problem

Don't leave good stuff outside overnight. It just encourages them.

One day, I parked in front of a local Fargo retailer. I won't get more specific than that, other than to say the owner sells both new and used items, and some of the things he buys and sells are quite valuable.

And, when the weather was good – it was sometime between May and September, that's all I remember about what time of year this incident took place – he'd put some of his less valuable, more durable items outside, in front of his building, so they could be seen from the road. During stretches of good weather, it seemed like he left the stuff out there for days at a time. I mean 24/7. He'd leave it outside until the weather was threatening to get bad.

There were quite a few things outside, in front of his establishment, this day, as I parked in front of his place.

I walked in. Didn't see the owner, who we'll call John (not his real name). I walked over to the separate part of his establishment where he keeps his more valuable stuff. I looked in there. No one. Lots of very valuable stuff, though.

I wasn't surprised. This had happened before when I'd come in looking for John. This guy was almost *too* Fargo.

And I was reminded of the recent visit Billy, Austen and I had made up to that high-tech industrial facility in northern Minnesota.

As I walked toward the back of the place looking for him, I realized I wanted to ask John a question that had nothing to do with the original purpose of my visit. I heard voices coming from a room off to the right. I headed in, and found John helping a customer bring some stuff he was buying to the front of the store.

"Oh, hi, Marc." He said as soon as he saw me.

"Hi, John! Need some help?"

No, I don't work for John. Never have. I just like the Fargo way of business, and part of it is that loyal customers offer to help out, when it seems appropriate.

"No, thanks, I think we got it." One of John's workers was doing what needed to be done. John was shaking hands with the customer, saying, "If it doesn't work out the way you need it to, just bring it back, and if you need anything else, just holler."

Now he was walking toward me. "How are booksales?"

"Pretty good, John. Thanks. I've got a question for you."

"Yeah? What's that?"

"Do you ever get any of that stuff stolen from out front, leaving it there overnight?"

"No, sometimes I wish I would, though, because what happens is I'll get here in the morning sometimes and there's new stuff out there, so it kind of builds up."

I started chuckling. "Oh, that's too Fargo. "Crappy stuff?"

"No! Good stuff! This morning there was a whole box of brand new [type of item], out there, somebody left it overnight, you know, never opened, never used, still in the original packaging, clean, quite an assortment, actually. So now I have to unpack it and sort it and price it and put the different things in the right places throughout the store."

"Well, John," I said, once my laughter subsided enough that I could talk, "What you have, it's safe to say, is a Fargo kind of problem."

"Yeah, you got that right, Marc."

Marc de Celle

18.

Fargo is on the Case

Help the victim and catch the bad guy.

Here are two well-written vignettes that give a pretty complete picture of how crime, and crime-solving, tends to work around here. In fact, I think it might have been these two stories that first gave me the idea I ought to include a section on true crime in this book.

When I was a junior at Concordia College in Moorhead, Minnesota, Fargo's "twin city" just across the Red River, it was my month to make the deposit into the bank of our out-of-town landlord. My roommates all had checking accounts, while I never really had enough money to warrant a checking account… so I gathered my $101.33, along with their checks, and put them in my backpack. Then I biked over to my 2-hour art class on campus, after which I planned to make the deposit.

I left my backpack while we went into the clay room to work on sculpture. After class, I pedaled down to the bank to make the deposit. But when I looked in my backpack, my wallet was gone! I was distraught. No money. My roommates could simply cancel payment on their checks. But I had no money for rent and parents who already had two kids in college on one Wisconsin teacher's salary. My tunnel vision reaction didn't allow me perspective on how I could survive this financial setback (in 1983, $100 was a lot of money to most college students).

I belonged to a campus club that had a meeting that night. I told my story to one of the 5th year seniors who listened and consoled me (Judy Seigle…a local Fargo Hero now).

One of the "non traditional" students in the group, who had gone to the Navy before college, saw my tears as I lamented to Judy… he asked "What's wrong, Smiley?" (Up to this point I was usually grinning, as my loans were allowing me to ignore my growing financial deficit!) Judy told him my story and he offered to pay my rent. I was brave/stupid and said "No, but thanks… I'll have to figure this out on my own." I went worrying on my way, trying to figure out how I was going to solve my money dilemma.

The next morning, I stopped by my PO Box (equivalent to checking facebook or email in this day and age) and found a white envelope in my box that said "Smiley" on the front. Upon opening it, I found a check made out to me with a note that said, "For your rent. Won't take no for an answer. Don't pay me back. Some day you will find someone who needs help. Pay them." ~Eric (This was LONG before the movie "Pay It Forward").

Eric was right. I have found many folks in my life who need help... and that $100 he shared with me has generated giving from my soul that found its roots in that timely gift.

The next year, my senior year, I got a phone call from a business a few blocks off campus. One of their workers had been working on some electrical issues in a false ceiling in a men's room on campus and had found my wallet. Everything was still intact... except my cash.

Another story: After a stint in Los Angeles... a grand adventure that had me relearning how to NOT trust humankind... I was offered a job back in the Fargo area, as a youth director at First Lutheran Church. One of my main tools in this career was my trusty Martin guitar... bought with money saved up during my years in L.A.

One day, after a brief trip from my office to the copy machine, I came back to realize that the place where my guitar normally stood was glaringly empty. Panic rising in my chest... I looked around... checked my Toyota... nope. Gone. What to do... tell someone... which I did. Panic... which I did. I called the police and let them know of my loss. They were sympathetic but this was, frankly, not a "Turn on the red lights, 1 Adam 12" moment. Next, I called the pawn shops in the area and let them know I was missing my Martin guitar. While all of the pawn shop workers were sympathetic and listened to my story when I called, one fellow in particular exclaimed, "You lost your Martin? Man, you must be bummin'!" He was obviously a guitar owner. "I haven't had a Martin come through here in three years. I'll be on the lookout."

I then set out on my own, driving around, looking for someone carrying my guitar case. No luck. When I came back to my office, slightly defeated by the loss of my single most valuable item (stealing my little red pickup would not have been as big of a deal as losing my guitar, as any seasoned artist will tell you), I had a message to call one of the pawn shops. The poor thief had chosen to sell my Martin to the pawn store owner who'd really understood my plight. The thief had wanted to sell that fine instrument for just $50! Later, the pawn store owner told me he knew it was mine before the kid even opened the case. He also told me he was tempted to ask the thief to play him a tune before he took his driver's license in the back to "write him a check," whereupon he actually called the cops and waited. As the kid was being apprehended, he called me to tell me the good news. I really wanted to hug that pawn store owner... he was glad to help, he was modest and friendly... and since then I've had a story I've shared all over the country at many gigs I've played... because every guitar has a story and my guitar has a very "How Fargo of you" legacy.

A previous guitar of mine (pre-Martin) was stolen from my office in North Hollywood, California. I never heard a word back from pawn shops or law enforcement. That was in 1986. I'm not holding my breath!

Rhoda Anderson Habedank, Twin Valley, Minnesota.

19.

The Answer

62.5%

A few days after I talked with State's Attorney for Cass County Birch Burdick, on a late Friday afternoon, his administrative assistant emailed me a computerized listing of convictions for murder in Cass County since 2000. I did an Internet search on every name on the list to learn their backgrounds.

But there were names and stories I could remember seeing and reading about in the news that weren't on the list. I began to understand what Deputy Chief Claus and Birch had been trying to tell me – this would be an incomplete reckoning of what I was looking for.

So I did a thorough Internet search, year-by-year, from 2000 forward, for any and all murder convictions in the region. I found four additional cases that hadn't been convicted in Cass County, but in adjoining counties. Here are the results of my investigation:

Five of the eight convictions for first degree murder in the Fargo region between January 2000 and October of 2013 were committed by people who had lived in our region for less than a year. So exactly 62.5% of the guilty verdicts for first degree murder here in this century were found against people who had spent less than a year in our area. (See Notes on the Chapters at the end of the book for full details.)

Somehow, all the while I was writing this chapter, I thought I'd be happy if it turned out I was right. But having spent a day poring through these cases, I'm not feeling particularly cheerful. I prefer the lighter side of Fargo immensely.

So let's get back to it. Let's find a happy crime to finish this off.

20.

True Fargo Graffiti

If you're going to break the law, break it the Fargo way.

A few summers ago, my daughter Anastasia and her friend Megan started occasionally rollerblading around Fargo and West Fargo. Coming in through the garage door after one of her early excursions with Megan, Anastasia made an excited announcement:

"Hey, dad, I saw my first Fargo graffiti today!"

"Really?" I asked. I couldn't remember ever seeing any graffiti in Fargo, except on the freight trains that roll through town from all parts of the country, east and west, on a regular basis.

"Yeah, it was in an underpass," Anastasia said, with a big grin starting to take over her face, "where the sidewalk curves down under the freeway, and it's really cool down there, and somebody painted these beautiful flowers and it says, right above the flowers,

'Stay Beautiful, Fargo!'"

In Closing

Goldilocks Zones

Just right for growing healthy communities.

In the new field of Astrobiology, scientists have coined the term *Goldilocks Zones* to describe planets where life might exist – not too close or too far from their home stars, so they're not too hot or too cold, not too big or too small, so their gravity isn't too strong or too weak, not rotating too fast or too slow, so the climate is fairly stable, with water, a magnetic field and all the other factors that might make a planet "just right" for life.

I'm going to borrow their term and speculate that the Northern Prairie region – from Iowa and Nebraska up into North Dakota and northern Minnesota, in the early 21st century, has a lot of little Goldilocks Zones for human culture.

The core culture has been forming for more than a century, since about the time Laura Engels Wilder was growing up in her family's Little House on the Prairie in South Dakota in the late 1800s. But until the Internet, these wonderful places were too isolated to foster or retain tremendous creativity.

Two years ago, I was talking with Mike Draper, a successful thirty-something entrepreneur and author of *The Midwest: God's Gift to Planet Earth*. He grew up in Des Moines, Iowa, and could hardly wait to get away. After graduating from college in Pennsylvania, he started a successful T-shirt business in the east and got married. Then they had a child, and he started wondering...

He's a very tech-savvy guy. He can run his business from his smartphone. And one day he realized he could have his cake and eat it too. His kids could have the best environment in the world to grow up in, and it wouldn't hurt his business one iota.

He and his wife moved to Des Moines. They got a storefront in downtown Des Moines and moved into the apartment above it. They were the first people to do that in 32 years. That was 2005, the same year we moved to Fargo. Now, that entire downtown block of Des Moines is full of thriving shops with owners living above them – other people who've done exactly what Mike and his wife did eight years ago.

This just scratches the surface of what's going on in this region. But the simple fact is, in the age of the Internet, people don't have to live in big cities anymore to find big opportunities.

So I suspect we're at the very beginning of a big change in the way people will live in our new century.

From Des Moines to Fargo; Appleton, Wisconsin, to Lincoln, Nebraska; Sioux Falls, South Dakota to Warroad, Minnesota, these changes are already starting – and the funny thing is, there are a lot of parallels between the way these old farming communities have always networked to survive, and the way the post-industrial economy of the Internet works.

This book barely scratches the surface of what's going on around here. I haven't written about how the annual crisis of winter and the ensuing, frequent spring floods have probably played a central role in the personality of this culture. These crises aren't constant, but they are regular – and they are almost always manageable, if just. They are Goldilocks Crises, bringing the community together, reminding everyone of their interdependence, but not – knock on wood – breaking the culture. So they serve to strengthen the culture, almost daily, at least six months out of the year.

I haven't written about the current high-tech leaders of the economy in the Red River Valley, many of whom were driving big grain trucks to market on back roads when they were ten or twelve years old. Or the fact that many of the people now in positions of leadership grew up on subsistence farms without electricity in their youth – through North Dakota winters, no less. A lot of these people have experienced two centuries of technological advance in their own lifetimes. And there are dozens of other amazing things I haven't even touched on yet, even though this is my second book about this Different Planet in America.

So another book is coming – *Goldilocks Zones of the Northern Prairie*, or something along those lines. I want stories not just from the Fargo area (although I want those too!) but also from anywhere and everywhere around here: Iowa, Nebraska, Wisconsin, South Dakota, Manitoba and beyond. Tell me the most amazing things you've seen and experienced, and what you think about them.

Please send your stories to marc@fargokind.com.

Thank you!

Notes on the Chapters

Introduction, What Planet Is This?

I found out Julia was a hairstylist, so now I'm a client. She does a great job, which is no surprise, is it? Julia Dobbins. You can find her on facebook.

Book I, Anonymous Kindness

Chapter 8, He Looked at Me Like I Was from Mars

Yes, frost boils can happen in June up here – a frost boil is where ice frozen below ground warms up and makes a muddy boil on the surface . If you've never seen one, I recommend doing a search for "frost boil" on You Tube.

Chapters 14-24 (Mayville stories)

I didn't include every story I heard around the semicircle. Some asked that theirs not be published, lest people "back home" get upset with them for talking about how much nicer people are in North Dakota, while a few other stories were nearly identical, in which case I chose just one.

Book II, The Fargo Way

Chapter 2, Go Far

Fargo held its first marathon in 2005, just a year before Jill's story took place. That race had less than 2,500 participants. Last year, less than a decade later, the 2013 Fargo Marathon boasted more than 24,000 participants, coming from all corners of the globe. The Fargo Marathon has now raised over $300,000 for local children's charities. The Fargo Way works.

Chapter 24, Interview with a Banker

The estimates of foreclosures from the subprime mess by the Pew Charitable trust are no longer online. The subprime mess appears to have largely run its course. You can now get actual foreclosure rates, state-by state. I like this site:

http://www.realtytrac.com/statsandtrends/foreclosuretrends/

As of this writing, mid-October 2013, according to this Realty Trac site, Washington, D.C. has the lowest foreclosure rate, month-to-month, with one in 42,216 homes being foreclosed on. Of the fifty states, North Dakota is lowest, with one in 39,440 homes being foreclosed on, Vermont second lowest, with one in 24,714 homes being foreclosed on. Mississippi and Montana are third and fourth, both with one in a little over every 15,000 homes being foreclosed on. All other states are more than double that rate except South Dakota, with one in every 7,849 homes being foreclosed on.

Here's a fun little video about Fargo's economy put together by CNN back in February, 2009, in the midst of the Great Recession:

http://www.cnn.com/video/#/video/us/2009/02/26/tuchman. what.recession.cnn

Book III, Zero Degrees of Separation – no notes

Book IV, True Fargo Crime

Chapter 3, Number Crunching

You can do all the simple crime research I describe here by going to these websites and scrolling down until you get to the table showing crime statistics and rates per 100,000:

Here's a website detailing Fargo crime statistics:
http://www.city-data.com/city/Fargo-North-Dakota.html

Here's a website detailing Phoenix crime statistics:
http://www.city-data.com/crime/crime-Phoenix-Arizona.html

Here's a website detailing Glendale, AZ crime statistics:
http://www.city-data.com/city/Glendale-Arizona.html

Chapter 4, To Protect and Serve

This conversation took place on August 26, 2013.

Chapter 12, Lock It or Lose It

I'm quoting this Fargo Police Department PSA from memory, and I'm sure I don't have it word-for-word verbatim. I think the police have a very good point with their PSA message, "Lock it or Lose it," even here in Fargo. In the eight years we've lived here, I can remember at least three different stretches – usually about a week long – when there was a rash of car thefts and things being stolen out of cars. In each instance, as I recall, it turned out to be a group of two or three teenagers who'd just started prowling around in the middle of the night, messing with all the unlocked cars everywhere. And in each instance, they were quickly caught.

The longest of these binges lasted two or three weeks before the kids were identified and apprehended. But if people had been locking their cars, I suspect none of these teens might have fallen into this pattern in the first place. I was a crazy 13-year-old boy once. I know firsthand how susceptible to impulse that species can be, and how, once started down a bad course, reason can just fly away like a dandelion on the wind until someone grabs you, gives you a good shake and brings you back to terra firma.

So I tend to think that removing temptation, whenever and wherever possible – as in locking your car – can be a very Fargo thing to do.

Chapter 16, When in Fargo

Balzer was a junior officer at the time, the other two pilots were the Captain and the First Officer on the flight. Balzer's book is about his struggles as a Christian to overcome his alcoholism and return to flying. According to his website, flyingdrunk.com, as of August 31, 2013, he's been sober for 19 years and has achieved the rank of Captain with American Airlines.

Chapter 18, Fargo is on the Case

In her first story, Rhoda mentioned that Judy Siegle was a "local Fargo hero now," so I checked it out:

From judysiegle.com: She was a high school basketball star with a promising college future. But in a split second, her life changed forever. Her dream of playing college basketball was shattered when a drunk driver sped through a stop sign near her hometown of Pelican Rapids, Minn. The car crash left her with a broken neck. At 18, she faced life in a wheelchair. But that's not the end of the story. "Back then I never would have dreamed I would be competing in sports at any level. I really thought my days in the competitive arena were done. What could a quadriplegic possibly do in sports other than be a spectator?" Judy Siegle

ATHELETIC ACCOMPLISHMENTS:

Judy Siegle went to become one of the elite wheelchair racers in the world, and she has the credentials to prove it:

- A member of the U.S. team in the 1996 Paralympics in Atlanta and the 2000 Paralympics in Sydney, Australia.
- Winner of two gold medals in the Mexico City PanAm Games, 1999.
- National record holder in the 400, 800, 1500 and 5000-meter events for quadriplegic women.
- Named 2000 Female Athlete of the Year by USA Wheelchair Track and Field.

Chapter 19, The Answer

First Degree Murder convictions in the Fargo region, 2000-October, 2013:

2004: James Allen Gunderson, 21, of West Fargo, ND and John Jacob Cooper, 25, of Fargo, ND, were convicted in the murder of David Hinojosa Jr., 22, of Dilworth MN; Lee Alexander Solarski, 21, of Moorhead, MN was convicted of aiding the offenders. In the midst of the meth epidemic here, this murder was over a small drug debt.

2006: Dennis James Gaede was convicted of the murder of Timothy Wicks of Gardner, ND; Gaede had just recently moved to North Dakota from Milwaukee with the intent of stealing Wick's identity, and then murdered Wicks when he discovered what was up.

2008: Sergei Issac Scott was convicted of murdering his sister; Scott had been adopted from Russia and had been living in Wisconsin with his adoptive father; he had only been in Fargo with his adoptive mother and sister for a very brief period when the murder occurred.

2009: Elijah Addai was convicted of the murder of David Delonais. In scouring all the articles I could find, I found nothing to the effect that Elijah was a recent transplant to the Fargo area, so I'm assuming he had lived here at least a year at the time of the crime.

2011: Michael Allen Nakvinda was convicted of the murder of Philip Gattuso, a dentist who had recently moved to Fargo. Nakvinda was a resident of Oklahoma who was found guilty of murdering Gattuso for $3000 paid him by fellow Oklahoman Gene Kirkpatrick, who was Gattuso's father-in-law. Kirkpatrick was later convicted of conspiracy to murder.

2011: Tracy Zornes was convicted of murdering Megan Londo and John Cadotte in Moorhead. Zornes lived in Naytahwaush, located in the middle of the White Earth Indian Reservation in Minnesota, just 80 miles northeast of the Fargo area, so I counted him as a convicted murderer from our region.

2011: Daniel Wacht was convicted of the murder of Kurt Johnson in Cooperstown, ND, about an hour northwest of Fargo. Wacht was from California and had just arrived shortly before the crime.

2013: Ronald Rogers was convicted of murdering his wife, Elizabeth, just six months after the two of them arrived in Fargo, having come from Idaho.

Those are all the First Degree Murder convictions I was able to find any hint of in the general Fargo region between 2000 and October 2013. But there are related crimes I did not include in my analysis:

In May of 2013, Henry Leo Deniger was found not guilty in the stabbing death of his wife, Kathy Deniger, by reason of insanity, although he allegedly confessed to the crime. The crime took place in March of 2012, in Fargo; various reports say the Denigers had moved to Fargo from Washington State anywhere from 9 to 18 months prior to the murder. All reports say that the couple had no prior connections to the Fargo area.

Lesser charges: All four attempted murder convictions in our region between 2000-October 2013 were committed by locals, as were most of the manslaughters and negligent homicides (these last were all auto or other accidents usually precipitated by drinking or drugs). I found no convictions for second degree murder 2000-October 2013.

This was not an exhaustive, scour-the-earth search. I spent a good day on the Internet after receiving the Cass County list, but not a week calling everyone under the sun and looking under rocks. I believe I got it right. If you know something I don't, or feel I have erred in this report, please email me at marc@fargokind.com, so I can improve later editions of this book. Thank you.

In Closing, Goldilocks Zones

Other Fargo statistics:

High school graduation rates: (U.S. News & World Report): http://www.usnews.com/education/best-high-schools/north-dakota

Bear in mind that the dropout rate in the western part of North Dakota, according to the North Dakota State Data Center, has increased about sixfold since the oil boom started, as fit young men have been able to walk out onto just about any oilfield in the west for the last few years and start making more than $20 an hour. But the state still has the second highest graduation rate in the nation, after Iowa.

Google "Fargo unemployment rate." Currently 3.2 as I write this. But this can be deceptive. There's twice or three times as much talent and work ethic here as anywhere else I've ever lived, so most of it ends up somewhat underemployed and, relative to other areas, underpaid (there's twice as much of it available, so it's not as valuable; basic economics). To get myself employed properly, I had to write a book. That, by the way, is also The Fargo Way. And it's sort of expected around here. Underemployed? Guess you better fix that.

Here's the latest interesting list as I write this, just came out in late October, 2013: The best places for young people, 18-24, to do well: North Dakota, followed by South Dakota and Nebraska. Also the three states that weathered the Great Recession the best, in terms of unemployment rates, in that order. No coincidence. Not for me. Same stuff that makes a place great for kids also makes for a stable economy.

Anyway, here's the list:

http://www.money-rates.com/research-center/best-states-for-young-adults/2013.htm

Final note: If you start Googling "Fargo best place" and similar phrases, you'll find enough lists from the last few years to make your head spin.

Marc de Celle is the author of *How Fargo of You*, the bestselling book about North Dakota of the 21st century. He speaks about Northern Prairie culture and consults on implementing the Fargo Way of business in various environments. His previous writings include the noted 2004 report *Anticipating Crisis*, which warned of accelerating risks to U.S. infrastructure well before these dangers were widely recognized, garnering accolades from leading scientists, authors and experts across a wide range of fields. For more information, visit www.fargokind.com.